THE WONDERS OF EUROPE

THE EDITORS OF RÉALITÉS

THE WONDERS OF EUROPE

Preface by Salvador de Madariaga

G. P. PUTNAM'S SONS, NEW YORK

All translation, reproduction and adaptation rights reserved for all countries including the USSR
First published in France in 1963 as **Les Merveilles de l'Europe**
© 1963 Librairie Hachette and Société d'Études et de Publications Économiques
This edition © 1964 Librairie Hachette and Société d'Études et de Publications Économiques
Published simultaneously in the Dominion of Canada by Longmans Canada Limited, Toronto
Library of Congress Catalog Card Number 64-23063
Printed in France

THE TEXTS ARE BY

GEORGES CHABOT,
PRESIDENT OF THE FRENCH NATIONAL
GEOGRAPHICAL COMMITTEE

PIERRE DE BOISDEFFRE

EDMOND POGNON,
KEEPER OF THE PRINT ROOM
IN THE BIBLIOTHÈQUE NATIONALE, PARIS

FRANÇOIS FONTAINE,
DIRECTOR OF THE INFORMATION OFFICE
OF THE EUROPEAN COMMUNITIES, PARIS

TABLE OF CONTENTS

S HE *made him small so as to make him carefully," Alfred de Musset wrote of Namouna's mother. This seems also to have been Nature's way when she gave forth the European Continent. The smallest in the planet, it is the most delicately planned, designed, modeled. If other continents solicit our wonder by the horizontal immensities of their vast plains and deserts or the vertiginous heights of their mountains, ours makes us marvel at the harmony and the sense of proportion in the shape of the whole and in its local conformations; and if elsewhere the scale is plane- tary, oceanic, lunar, it is in our continent intimate and, as it were, in keeping with the size of our homes.*

A continent which abounds in inner seas, it seems to take pleasure in grouping the riparian peoples around a common sea-center, like neighbor- ing families around the Main Square, every man in his home, of course, yet all in a common "home" in which, with the aid of time, lives are woven together into rich traditions which the mixture of local colors renders irides- cent, like those old cloths which grandmothers now and then bring out from the depths of their coffers.

The chains of mountains, the rivers and the seas trace on its terri- tory barriers formidable enough to define separate environments, homes in which, isolated from their neighbors, its several peoples find through the cen- turies leisure enough to shape for themselves a soul and a body of such spiri- tual force that, by merely looking at them, even before we have heard them speak or taken in the style of their gestures, we cry out: a Neapolitan, a Dutchman, a Breton, an Andalusian! Yet Europe's seas, rivers, mountains have never opposed an inexorable wall to the passage of men and ideas: so that the continent has ever been the venue of a dialogue between peoples different enough to wish to exchange views, yet related closely enough to be able to meet and communicate in a common idiom.

Moderate dimensions, clear lines, the never violent play of plains and heights, rivers and their gradients, forests, pastures and the lands which the plow has combed, villages of houses huddled together around their churches like herds around their shepherds—all this spontaneous, vigorous life flourishes in an atmosphere of natural peace and harmony.

A few clear facts seem to have determined the destiny of the continent. A frame of mountains defines it: to the north, the Scandinavian crystalline system; to the south, the tablelands and the chains of heights which, through the Alps, the Carpathians and the Balkans, connect the Iberian with the Anatolian castle; to the east, the barrier of the Urals. Within this frame, a vast plain spreads which, starting from Aquitaine, stretches over the west and north of France and covers the whole northern region of the continent. Rising above this plain, the Swiss Alpine system gives forth the three great European rivers, the Danube, the Rhine and the Rhône, three spokes of an immense wheel. One flows toward the east, threading a rosary of varied nations which it unites in a common tradition; the second flows northward to become the frontier and the link between the Latin and the Germanic peoples, pointing its outlet toward the British Isles, countries which, as every other on either bank of this river, remain undecided between the Latin and the Germanic worlds; finally, the third, having first flown northward, turns toward the Mediterranean and becomes the Roman river par excellence. Toward the south, the continent juts toward Africa its three peninsulas, Greece, Italy and Spain; toward the west, its three universal countries, Britain, France and Spain-Portugal.

It is all so familiar that the Europeans hardly notice it any longer. But let the son of Europe venture afar and, out of his native environment, he will soon realize how distinct are the features common to the whole continent. He will remember how nature respects, even among plants and animals, those harmonious proportions which the European embodies in the landscapes of his countrysides and in the architecture of his cities; and he will come to think that if in Europe one hears much about the differences which distinguish and at times separate the Europeans, out of Europe one is apt to dream of those silent, profound things which are common to us all, from Dublin to Athens, from Helsinki to Lisbon, from Paris to Moscow.

The will to be oneself, the wish to learn all about oneself and the world, the spirit of enterprise and discovery, the thirst for freedom, the demand that faith, as it wells up from the heart, be clarified by a filter of reason, a *taste for the simple and the natural, an attitude of equality toward women (too depressed in the East, too exacting in the West), a sense of quality which no quantity could satisfy, and a sense of the work truly achieved, the inner failure of which no outward success could veil—these are some of the features which have made of Europe the leading continent in man's history.*

Sta viator.   Heroem calcas.

How not to recall this epitaph when thinking of our Europe! At every step on her soil we tread on earth made fertile by the ashes of history.   It is here, in this city rich in venerable ruins, that Socrates lived; it is here, close to the corner of the European finis terrae, *that the pilgrimage ended in honor of St. James the Apostle; it is here, in this tiny harbor, that the three caravels bade farewell to Europe and sailed away to discover a new world; it is here, in this austere cabinet, that Copernicus restored order to men's ideas about the sky; it is here, in this cool garden, that Linnaeus received his intuition of the order that rules the world of plants; it is here . . . it is here . . . it is here . . . .*

There are regions in Europe—Florence, Rome, Paris—the mere name of which calls forth constellations of great ancestors.   But how many cities of Europe draw honor from the name of a great man whom luck bestowed on them?   Shall we recall Rotterdam who gave us Erasmus, Eisenach which gave us Bach, Chinon which gave us Rabelais, Vinci where Leonardo was born, Woolthorpe where Newton came into the world? So many others scattered all over Europe? Yet, what better symbol of all these mother cities of genius than the name of the village where Goya was born: Fuendetodos, the fount of all.   A handsome name for Europe.

Salvador de MADARIAGA

NATURE

BY

GEORGES CHABOT

Europe—and above all western Europe—that "poor little cape" tacked on to the Asian continent! Men through the ages have delighted in thus humbling the pride of the Europeans, who like to believe they are at the heart of the world.

But what a cape! And how well it is situated! It is equidistant from the equator and the North Pole, from the perpetually lush forests of the tropics and the permanently icebound seas of the Arctic. And what a profusion of climates and vegetations! In the north of Europe lie the forests of conifers and birches, indefinite and haunting like the forests of Siberia or Canada; yet they have their almost domestic charm when the light plays through the foliage of the birches, or in autumn when the rust of deciduous leaves veneers the dark green of the conifers with its yellows and browns. By contrast, in the south of Europe, the Mediterranean lands already call to mind the arid deserts of Africa; trees varnish their leaves and reduce them to mere thorns the better to resist the heat; rich plants swell themselves with reserves against thirsty times; laurel and cactus abound; gray tints dominate among the foliage of the olive trees; grass is scarce and in summer even the hardy sheep must seek pasture elsewhere. Between these two extremes lies the Europe of meadows and woods, with its abundant variety of greens, able to moderate the rigors both of winter and of summer, generous to man despite its uncertain climate.

And then, this cape projects into the Atlantic Ocean at the most favorable point, in a veritable gulf of warmth. The ocean is in fact crossed, southwest to northeast, by a current that mantles it like a shawl, carrying right up to the Scandinavian coastline the waters that have been warmed in the torrid latitudes of Florida; in winter it spreads its protective warmth around the European cape. Ships can navigate in permanently ice-free waters around all the British ports; in Iceland, on the fringe of the Arctic Circle, the average temperature of the coldest month in Reykjavik rarely falls below freezing—while at the same latitude ice covers vast stretches of North America. It is miraculous to see lights blazing, in January, in Oslo, Stockholm and Helsinki, witnessing the intense human activity there, while in Labrador, at the same distance from the pole, Eskimos are huddling in their igloos. And while people shiver in New York, Naples basks in its bay under the sun's rays. A choice place in the world has indeed been reserved for Europe.

It would seem that Europe has always been conscious of the privileges conferred upon it by its advanced position in the Atlantic, and that it has striven to take the maximum profit from it; to this end, it multiplied its contacts with the ocean and took advantage of the bordering seas that really extend the continent: the Mediterranean, the English Channel, the North Sea and the Baltic. The cape seems to unravel in peninsulas: the Iberian, Italian, Balkan, Scandinavian. Islands broke away, the better to profit by the ocean which opened the routes of the British Empire; Corsica, Sardinia, Sicily and the Balearic Islands were scattered in the Mediterranean; and far off, near Greenland, Iceland rose out of the tepid sea.

So emerges the maritime, outgoing character of Europe, in contrast to the self-contained massiveness of other continents. The shoreline of Europe is quite varied: now it falls into the sea in sheer cliffs, as in Normandy; now it is infiltrated by creeks, estuaries and fjords. Elsewhere, long sandy beaches stretch out, or there are the amphibious landscapes of the North Sea, where water and land are so close together that they almost merge.

But to understand them well, we must relate these shores with the lands they border.

If Europe opens itself so widely to the maritime influence, it is because it presents itself in slices, as it were. It is formed by successive strips, running east-west, that appeared one after another, and each of which corresponds to a belt of the earth's crust. In microcosm it is the whole structure of the Northern Hemisphere, and marks its abrupt plunge into the Atlantic Ocean where this structure was swallowed up in circumstances that remain mysterious. One can distinguish a northern Europe, a middle Europe and a southern Europe.

The most northern regions, Scotland and its islands, and especially Scandinavia, are formed of the oldest rocks, those formed at the dawn of geological time. Their age is reckoned in hundreds of millions of years; and they have undergone many changes. Long and patient erosions demolished them or wore them down: but new convulsions of the earth's crust cast them up anew and restored their mountainous aspect. In the course of these rude ordeals the rocks were compressed into hard, compact masses which seem to defy all attacks today. It is to show their rigidity that geologists have compared this base to a shield—the Baltic shield. Around the Baltic, in eastern Sweden and in Finland, it forms low plateaus that slope seaward, cut by the Swedish rivers which flow in parallel valleys. A single vast rift valley stretches from Stockholm down to Göteborg; it is garnished with lakes and is Sweden's most heavily populated area.

But a part of this base was raised up to form the Scandinavian range, the long mountain mass straddling Sweden and Norway, that falls sheer down to the Norwegian coast. Here is an often monotonous upland; these old massifs have been planed down so often that they have become dowdy; their greatest heights are under 8,200 feet, but a few thousand feet are sufficient in these Nordic regions for vegetation to wilt. On the *fjälls* it is reduced to a few stunted birches, dwarf willows and lichen; patches of snow survive all summer, and some peaks even have small glaciers. The northern portion of this range is the domain of the Lapps, small men inseparable from the immense herds of reindeer they drive before them. After wintering in the plains, they make for the mountains in spring, covering hundreds of miles and pitching their tents at each stage of the journey. The Scottish Highlands, with their moors and their half-wild sheep, parallel these Scandinavian landscapes.

At times, in the northwest, nearer to the convulsions of the Atlantic, volcanic eruptions created some strange landscapes. Lava covered the white chalk of Antrim in Ireland with a black mantle. At times it solidified into huge prisms, their massed summits like a giant's flagstone walk. Iceland is unique, a block of lava continually shaken by new eruptions —like that of Hekla in 1947. There we have a true museum of volcanic forms, poured forth and congealed: craters garnished with lakes, pillars like organ pipes. Waters heated in the bowels of the earth spurt out in jets of steam, the geysers; they are tamed to supply heat for the towns or hothouses for flowers and vegetables. The phenomenon is all the more striking because of the glaciers that cover the highest parts of the land; fire and ice rub shoulders and volcanoes even burst into life under the glaciers, thawing them and provoking breakups that are often catastrophic.

If the old Scandinavian landscape seems a survival of the most distant times, it was also affected by one of the most recent geological phenomena. During the quaternary era, when man already existed, it was covered by the gigantic glacier that encircled the pole. A thickness of several thousand feet of ice covered everything, crushing the country with its weight, under which even the earth's crust yielded in certain places. Glaciers smoothed all projections, polished rocks, widened passages and deepened valleys. The Finnish plateau was converted into a series of little rounded domes and hollows in which thousands of lakes now sleep. On the Norwegian coast, ice, sculpturing the ancient valleys, prepared the fjords that the sea was to invade. There, ships sail between sheer, towering walls, and the little harbor towns have barely room to nestle. The after-effects of this glaciation are still going on today. The earth's crust, which sank under the covering of ice, has been slowly rising again since it was freed; and the coastline is tending to dry up. Even since Christian times, many ports have had to change their positions and pursue the retreating sea; at Stockholm the earth is still rising sixteen inches every hundred years.

It is in these Nordic regions of Europe that man's kinship with the sea is probably closest. The continent here has been broken into small pieces by the coastal waters, and the resultant fringe of islands is made of hard rock that resists the assault of the waves. Scotland is prolonged by the Hebrides, the Orkneys and the Shetlands; all along the Norwegian coast mountainous islands lie close off the shore; this fringe is continued with the Lofoten Islands and the Vesterålen Islands right up to the North Cape which stands as an advance guard in the Arctic Ocean. The Swedish and Finnish coasts of the Baltic Sea are girded with low islands, the "seed-bed of reefs," which cover the sea to such an extent that on a level with the Åland Islands one might think by looking at the map that one could cross the Baltic by leaping from island to island.

So it is in no way astonishing that maritime life developed to such an extent all over northern Europe, creating whole nations of fishermen and navigators. Descendants of the Vikings, the men of the North who sowed terror along European coasts, sailing far south in their longships, these nations have remained nations of sailors. This is especially true in Norway; along the North Sea, where fish abound, almost everyone is something of a fisherman. Primarily they fish for herring and cod; at the end of winter the fishing fleets gather in the northernmost islands, which, like the Lofotens, bustle with a hectic seasonal life.

To the south of this Scottish and Scandinavian Europe lies the strip of middle Europe, from Bohemia to Ireland. Its geological structure is due to the convulsions that, at the end of the primary period, threw up the mountains of Bohemia, the Harz Mountains, the schistose Rhine mass, the Vosges, the French Massif Central, the Armorican mass, Cornwall and the south of Ireland. Here the scenery is more varied than in Nordic Europe, the landscape less continuous and less uniform. The rocks are more varied; these were still under water when only northern Europe was visible above the surface; and within them are the precious layers of coal that man was to seek out in the very bowels of the earth. Thus were formed the "black regions" of England, Belgium, Flanders, Lorraine and the German Rhineland. The landscape is dominated by the structures that tower gauntly above the pits, and by the factories that compete to make use of this coal, still a vital source of power. Since their formation, these mountains have had their ups and downs; they were worn down several times, flattened, only to rise up again. Vast plateaus like that of the Limoges region give us some idea of those level planes on which only a few outcrops of harder rocks, more resistant to erosion, remain. This aspect occurs again and again throughout middle Europe. A rounded mountaintop in the Vosges, a peak in the Bohemian forest, a Breton landscape, all exhibit these vast, monotonous stretches of flatness.

But the entire unit was less rigid than the old Nordic masses; it was also closer to the great convulsions that rent the Mediterranean regions. And these mountains were broken up and faulted into several pieces; the schistose Rhine mass is actually only a mosaic of masses: Hunsrück, Taunus, Westerwald, Eifel and the Ardennes. In the same way, southern Ireland, Cornwall and the Armorican mass are a vast, continuous series of folds stretching from Ireland to the Massif Central, in France.

These faults stirred the eroded mountain masses; blocks were raised and toppled to form asymmetrical mountains. Germany's Harz Mountains slope gently in the south; but in the north they rear up, and their sudden appearance above the plain so struck the imaginations of the people that they took the Brocken (3,747 feet high) for an abode of supernatural beings. Likewise, the Vosges in Lorraine rise gradually toward their crest in the east, although their western, or Alsatian, slope is abrupt. The Massif Central, in France, rises sharply in the Cévennes, facing the Alps. We must also set apart certain landscapes. When we cross the limestone plateaus of the Massif Central, we see no water courses on their surfaces; the rivers run through them as strangers, at the bottom of narrow canyons. Rain water infiltrates into limestone fissures, widens them, hollowing out gulfs and running underground to create vast caverns in which lace patterns of stalactites hang; then the water disappears mysteriously to reappear in the large streams of the surrounding valleys. The exploration of these caves often results in exciting and dangerous escapades; spelunkers slip through narrow passages, cross lakes and face waterfalls and rock slides. Throughout Europe other similar limestone scenery can be found, in the Ardennes and the Swabian Jura, for example.

Amid these eroded and unimposing hills bolder shapes emerge, which almost seem to have been factory-made. They appeared much later, when masses of lava spread across the earth's crust, building strange reliefs—enormous volcanoes like the Vogelsberg in Germany, which covers some 800 square miles, or series of craters like the more recent *puys* (peaks) of Auvergne. It is among these volcanic forms that we find the highest peaks of middle Europe (the Puy de Sancy, 6,187 feet). Yet they are exceptions. They are extinct now, and the underground phenomena are no longer to be seen save in the thermal springs that feed spas.

On the whole, these middle European masses are gentle mountains; most of them do not reach 3,000 feet. If they once bore a few glaciers, whose amphitheaters now shelter the lakes of the Vosges, few traces of this can now be seen. They are hospitable mountains, on whose slopes men and their flocks are welcome.

They are all the more hospitable since they are interrupted by many plains. These mountains are most often composed of isolated masses, between which man can move easily. Faults opened up rift valleys in them, like the one through which the Rhine flows, between the Vosges and the Black Forest, or like Limagne, in the middle of the Massif Central. The mountains have always been of great value to the plains that penetrate them. Flocks graze on their rounded summits; the forests that cover them assure a supply of wood, and Paris warmed itself for a long time with logs brought down by the rivers of the Morvan. These well-watered mountains are also veritable water towers; torrents used to make machinery work, and today the dams on the rivers dispense electricity. Finally, the mountains were reservoirs of men; it was the emigration of the mountain-dwellers that populated the nearby plains and furnished labor for their factories in the industrial age. In addition, vast regions escaped the folds and the convulsions and formed plains. We must first set aside the great plain that separates northern Europe from middle Europe, prolonging the Russo-Polish plain. It extends through Denmark, Germany, the Netherlands and Belgium. The substratum, the old layers of land, are scarcely visible at all. Everything disappeared under the enormous mass of pebbles, sand and clay that the glaciers from Scandinavia spread as far as the Rhine. Then rivers washed through these moraines, causing the wide valleys which divide them today. So in the pulverized soil of these regions projections are few, rarely reaching 650 feet. Seen from the air, roads unfold like straight ribbons, broken only by occasional cloverleaf intersections. The lowest-lying, still poorly drained regions, are marshes; they form the southern coasts of the North Sea, the Low Countries, which are prolonged by islands lying almost at sea level. Man here strives to drain them and protect them by dikes; he wrests his soil from the sea, enclosing bays and transforming them into arable polders; but on these uncertain shores, the struggle against the waters is unceasing; it is crowned by magnificent

conquests, but is also set right back from time to time by terrible and seemingly inevitable catastrophes.

This belt of plains seems to extend farther west still; in reality, though, the London and Parisian basins are quite different. They constitute a unit which the sea bisects, with similarities on both sides of the English Channel; one finds the same cliffs at Newhaven that one left at Dieppe. Yet the London basin and the Parisian basin form two separate hollows; in each, lesser rivers converge on a main river, the Thames and the Seine, which are the axes of the basins. It is as if nature prepared the future of those two splendid capitals, London and Paris, by having vast regions converge upon them. It is the variety of the terrain that makes the variety of the landscapes, the limestone strata form hills that are breached by the valleys of the Moselle, the Meuse and the Ile-de-France; it is on their well-exposed slopes that the grapes ripen in Champagne. The most friable chalk gives the most blunted reliefs, the English downs, the plains of Champagne and the Norman plateaus; sands bear forests like that of Fontainebleau; clay, heavier and moister, is covered with meadows.

The variety of terrain has its equivalent in the variety of the coastal strips: chalk gives promontories that fall into the sea in white cliffs, as at Caux and Boulogne, at Dover and Newhaven; sands and clay are invaded by the sea and form gulfs. And the vast estuaries herald the prosperity of inland ports like London and Rouen.

These extensive plains, closely connected, have provided culture and industry with the favorable conditions that are the strength of middle Europe. On these plains man early established himself; he began to cultivate them in prehistoric times with his primitive stone tools. Many of the characteristics of our country districts were inherited from these distant ancestors; by gathering together at the center of their lands they fixed the sites of many if not most of today's villages.

But, spreading out from these villages as the population increased, man settled and reclaimed the forests. And then, in the lands near the Atlantic, the "hedge-row" system developed: farms are dispersed over the country and each field is surrounded by thick hedges between which creep muddy roads. At the center of a typical community of this kind stand a church, the town hall, the smithy and a few shops. The big domains, often former properties of lords, alternate with the thin strips of the fields, split up and decimated over the centuries by peasant legacies. The farmhouses, too, are extremely varied. Their walls indicate the material resources of the region: stone in limestone districts, clay or mud strengthened by wooden crosspieces in clay districts. Roofs are made of flat stones, tiles or slates, and slope more

steeply in the wintry North than in the milder South. The harsh reliefs and bold forms that erosion has not yet had time to grind down are almost nonexistent in northern Europe, rare in middle Europe; but they make up practically the whole of southern Europe. Admittedly the region has its plateaus and its masses of ancient rock, in the Iberian peninsula, in Provence, in Calabria, in Corsica and Sardinia; these are conspicuous by their coasts, which are festooned with little bays which narrow creeks prolong like the fingers of a glove. But such isolated masses are lost in the midst of mountain groups thrown up by extremely violent convulsions.

Honor where honor is due. The Alps unfold in a semicircle from the Mediterranean to the Danube. With their highest peaks exceeding 15,000 feet, they tower above the rest of Europe. The Alpine water tower feeds the Rhône, the Po, the Rhine and the Danube, flowing toward the Mediterranean, the North Sea and the Black Sea. All of these waters, which pour down the sides of the Alps, have carved out deep courses. So the Alpine valleys form a world apart amid the splendid peaks that are there for mountaineers to scale. The powerful glaciers of bygone days gave them this look of sheer-sided troughs; the glaciers of today and the melting snows assure them an abundant supply of water in summer, as well as floods in spring.

These valleys house a large population of mountain dwellers. Well sheltered, they support delicate cultivation, vines and fruit trees. Men, fearing the frequent floods, have set up hamlets on the slopes, using shelves and terraces. In the more verdant northern Alps they send their stock in summer to graze on the heights, now clear of snow. Along the many torrents, water power has given life to factories in Austria, Germany, Switzerland and France. And the beauty of these wild regions annually attracts tourists, multiplying chalets and enhancing the world-wide reputation of Innsbruck, Interlaken and Chamonix. The vogue for the snowfields added a winter season to the summer one; the Alps have become one of Europe's favorite holiday resorts. Lakes dot the foothills of the Alps, their deep waters reflecting the towering mass of the surrounding mountains. Mont Blanc overlooks Lake Geneva and the lakes of Savoy or Switzerland, embedded in the mountain sides. On the Italian slopes the gentleness of the climate lines the shores with orange trees and adds a Mediterranean touch to Lake Maggiore, Lake Como and Lake Garda.

But the Alps are not the sole relic of the convulsions that threw them up; that began with the Pyrenees, a long and defiant barrier between France and Spain.

And, of course, ramifications of mountains prolong the mass of the Alps themselves in all directions.

In the north, the Franco-Swiss Jura aligns its parallel ranges. To the south, the Apennines snake down into Sicily; the range is so young that volcanoes still smoke there — Vesuvius, Etna and Stromboli; rocks are often still so soft there that they crumble, and in certain places building is impossible. The Apennines are the backbone of the whole Italian peninsula. The other shore of the Adriatic is outlined by the mountains of Dalmatia. Here the limestone is more than 3,000 feet thick and water, dissolving it like sugar, has pierced it with multiple cavities before infiltrating into the ground, leaving behind basins that are completely isolated from one another. The sea, slipping among the mountains, confers a striking beauty on them; islands run parallel to the shores and gulfs penetrate deeply into the land, making the many-fingered Bay of Kotor one of the most striking landscapes in the world

This southern fringe of Europe is almost entirely composed of mountains set around seas, and plains are rare here. A furrow separates the Alpine world of middle Europe, stretching from the Pyrenees to Vienna, by the corridor of the Rhône, Bresse and the valley of the Danube; it broadens only in the Aquitaine basin and Bavaria.

The sea's edge is also dotted with small plains; they fringe it with marshy coasts, graded flat by the currents: Andalusia, the French Landes, Mediterranean Languedoc, the Italian Adriatic coast and the lagoons of Venice.

Men huddle together on these tiny coastal plains, perching their villages upon hillocks to avoid the marshes and the dangers of invasion and unsure coasts; there they grow the vines celebrated since antiquity. Ports have multiplied along the shores, fishing ports and trading ports, and some of them, like Genoa and Venice, once extended their power far across the sea.

But to the north and south of the Alps there are vast plains which are strewn with enormous masses of debris which have been torn from the mountains and deposited there. In the Swiss plateau, between the Jura and the Alps, and in the plain of the Po, the Alpine and Apennine debris meet. The glaciers brought much of it when they overflowed onto the neighboring plains, carpeting the Dombes with clay, depositing on the Bavarian plateau moraines which the rivers have since spread out. So even the plains are tributaries of the mountains, in this Europe that is dominated by the Alps.

Norwegian fjords chiseled from the Scandinavian mountains, islands sown along the Dalmatian coast, snow-covered Scandinavian *fjälls,* the mysterious Lorelei rising above the waves of the Rhine, ever-secretive underground caves, hallucinating peaks in the Alps. All these represent many wonders, and many of the finest of them will be found on the following pages. But the greatest wonder is probably the gathering together of all these landscapes within such a limited space. "The little European cape," in which such widely varied zones taper out and die, is an epitome of the earth's landscapes. And the use men have made of it, is not that another—and perhaps even a greater—wonder?   G. C.

THE COASTS

An azure shrine

washed

in eternal beauty...

Ancient Greece left her mark, in the form of these five columns standing on a stylobate and topped by a frieze, on the promontory of Sounion, at the southernmost tip of Attica. A naval base, standing at the entrance to the Saronic Gulf and the Euboean Channel, Cape Sounion served as an observation post for the Hellenic fleet, covering the flank of the Greek armies which fought Xerxes' forces. Fortifications protected the Acropolis, at the top of which stood a temple built in the second half of the fifth century B.C. and dedicated to Poseidon, god of the sea. The neighboring bay was used for peacetime naval competitions during the lesser Panathenaea.

Cape Sounion, Greece. ▶

where works of art

rise in

stone and marble...

Isle of Delos, Greece.

The dawn of a miracle can be seen in the serene power of this stone goddess which stands facing the sea on the island of Delos. For it was indeed a miracle which saw the rise, within the space of three centuries on the favored soil of ancient Greece, of one of the most perfect expressions of art. Legend has it that Poseidon thrust Delos up from the sea so that Leto, loved by Jupiter and pursued by her rival Juno, might have a place to give birth to Apollo and Artemis. Henceforth no mere mortal was allowed to die or be born on the sacred isle. The mortally ill and women in labor were taken to the nearby island of Reneia.

Walls of slumbering lava would have been the ideal lair for Vulcan, the blacksmith of the gods. The island of Santorin, called Thera in ancient times, was originally only a volcano of marble and metamorphic schist. On the inner curve of the crescent it forms, this cliff rises sheer for some 850 feet. Scoria, red and black volcanic ash, lava, and pumice stone lie superimposed in regular layers. No tree, no spring relieves the stark slopes of this ever-threatening volcano. Yet, perhaps in compensation, its ashes nurture vines that yield a heady and justly-famed wine.

◀ Isle of Santorin, Greece.

...an admirable haven for the sweetness of life...

Amalfi, Italy.

Isle of Capri, Italy. ▶

Towers and fishing nets sum up Amalfi past and present. Massive towers clinging to the rocks recall the Moorish raids on the Amalfi coast. It was in this flourishing maritime republic, the rival of Genoa and Pisa, that the earliest known code of the sea was drawn up in the thirteenth century. Here, too, the legend runs, Flavio Gioja invented the mariner's compass. The largest and finest galleys of the age were built in the shipyards of Amalfi. Today, fishermen repair their nets on its beaches.

Capri, famed through the ages, was visited in ancient times by the Emperor Augustus, then by the Emperor Tiberius, who built the Villa Jovis, in which he spent the last ten years of his life. The limestone needles piercing the smooth face of the sea are the "Faraglioni," a prolongation of Cape Tragara. Lying off Sorrento, at the entrance to the Gulf of Naples, Capri—"island of goats"—owes its great reputation as much to its gentle climate as to the rich variety of colors it presents to the sun.

... the Mediterranean coast,

stippled by sun

and shadow...

A legendary Titan's ax seems to have hewn this passage to the sea and one of those hidden coves or "calanques" of the coast of Provence (here, the Calanque d'En-Vau). The soft light which filters through the trees and plays on the water adds to the illusion that here is a real-life counterpart to the charm of a Debussy reverie. Only a few minutes from Marseilles, away from the noise and fumes of traffic, it provides twelve miles of peaceful sanctuary in which the modern city dweller can pretend he is Robinson Crusoe.

The Calanque d'En-Vau, near Cassis, France.

Gulf of Taormina, Sicily.

Stromboli, Italy. ▶

... sets the rise of civilization against the blind forces of nature.

Headlands laden with ancient ruins dominate the Gulf of Taormina, where the past has left its mark on each hill, and the Mediterranean light bathes a gentle landscape. Above the ruins of this city, founded at the beginning of the fourth century B.C., Etna's profile rises to 10,741 feet above sea level. As the pilots of antiquity neared the coast, they could make out, as can the modern voyager, the clear swell of farmlands on the lower slopes, the dark mass of forests higher up, and finally the shining black crater at the summit of the volcano, topped with snow.

A menacing—but harmless—old sea monster, Stromboli regularly spits out limited quantities of the lava that boils inside it and reaches almost to the lip of its crater. At night, single-handed, it organizes its own fireworks display. The sight of a stream of molten lava snaking down a crevasse into the sea is one of the most impressive in the world. On the slopes of Stromboli, inhabited since prehistoric times, men have hung their little square white houses and accustomed themselves to the dull rumble of the sporadic eruptions. They have planted vines which yield malmsey wine.

Basilica of St. Donatus, Zadar, Yugoslavia.

Eastern and Western Christianity meet in the Basilica of St. Donatus, built on the foundations of a Roman forum. The basilica was begun in the ninth century and finished in the thirteenth, and is one of the oldest medieval buildings in Dalmatia. As austere and grandiose inside as it is outside, it houses some of Carpaccio's most beautiful works in the darkness of its vaults. Like scars of its long history, one finds incorporated in its construction Roman pillars salvaged by the builders from the surrounding countryside, traces of a baroque restoration in the eighteenth century, and breaches opened by the 1944 bombings.

The ardor,

the gentle music,

of a meandering coastline...

Hemmed in between sea and mountain, the fishermen's villages along the Dalmatian coast suffer alternately, according to the season, from the heat of summer and the cold of winter, but poverty is present all the year round. Behind the double-glazed windows, between the walls of stone and dried mud, a simple patriarchal life has gone on unchanged for centuries, and is still largely untouched by modern civilization. A fierce wind, similar to the mistral, blows along these Adriatic shores which lie drowsing far from the great trade currents of the Mediterranean.

Stara Baska, Isle of Krk, Yugoslavia. ▶

"Gardians" of the Camargue, France.

Last realm where the horse is still king, the sandy soil of the Camargue has been given over to the "gardians," the brothers of the American cowboy, since the beginning of the nineteenth century. On some 12,500 acres of prairie, they raise their "manades" —herds of half-wild bulls destined for the bullring—and try to preserve the race of gray horses which, they say, are the descendants of those the Saracen invaders left behind when they swept through Provence in about the year 950.

...is a timeless attraction to the beasts

of the field and the birds of the air...

A fluttering cloud of pink, flamingos punctuate the untamed yellow plain of the Camargue with their strange silhouettes. Around the vast lagoon of Vaccarès, which, with its plumed reeds and water plants, offers an extraordinary landscape, an important botanical and zoological reserve has been created. It covers some 33,500 acres, and is a paradise for beavers, cormorants, ibises, cranes, egrets and storks.

Flight of pink flamingos, Camargue, France. ▶

A land of mirages, the Camargue still spreads its untrammeled horizons on which the spectator cannot tell where the sea begins, the sky approaches, or the land ends. The "gardians" spend the nights in these thatched huts, whose special feature is that they have no openings on the sides exposed to the mistral. Numerous outstanding writers, composers, and poets have sung the praises of this warm, murmuring land that has remained one of the last natural retreats available to man in southern Europe.

Perpetuating the miracle of hope, the pilgrimages to Saintes Maries de la Mer annually attract throngs in which believers and nonbelievers rub shoulders. In May, bands of gypsies in caravans, some still drawn by horses, gather at Saintes Maries. The procession honors the gypsies' patron saint, Sarah the Egyptian, "the Black Virgin." Later they worship at the shrines of Mary Salome and Mary Jacoba, who, according to a local legend, reached Provence 2,000 years ago in Lazarus' boat —without aid of sails, rudder or oars, accompanied by Martha and Mary Magdalene, Maximinius, Sidonius, and the serving girls Marcella and Sarah. After the procession to the sea and the benediction, the relics of the two saints are once again shut away in the chapel, where for another year they will watch over the people of the Camargue.

...and keeps alive ritual,

tradition,

pilgrimage.

Standing out from the horizon of moving sand, sea and cloud, the sturdy shape of the fortified church of Saintes Maries rises high above the sun-gnawed tiles of the surrounding roofs. Erected from 1140 to 1180 to replace a chapel originally built by the two saints on the ruins of a pagan temple, the church became too small for the flocks of pilgrims attracted by the relics which King René discovered there in 1448. At the end of the fifteenth century, the two west bays were added. The apse is surmounted by a thirteenth-century watchtower with an archway and belfry, built in the fifteenth century, which gives the church its warlike appearance. When invasion threatened, the inhabitants of Saintes Maries took refuge within its walls.

Gypsies in the church of Saintes Maries de la Mer, France.

The Lagoon of Venice, Italy.

A land of endless, melancholy reaches.

An amphibious world of mud and salt water, the Lagoon of Venice marks the north-western limits of the Adriatic. The ebbing tide leaves its debris behind, the rivers add their alluvial deposits whose accumulations would soon have filled the canals that are the charm—and the fortune—of Venice. As early as 1143, the Venetians went to war with Padua because that city had altered the course of the Brenta in their direction. They thrust its estuary back toward the south and deflected the Sile, which also threatened their insularity, to the north. But then the strip of land separating the lagoon from the sea was worn dangerously thin; the Lido had to be strengthened with sea walls, and at the same time channels had to be cut through to allow the sea access.

◀ Corfu, Greece.

"Island of the dead" the Swiss artist Arnold Böcklin called the picture he was inspired to paint on seeing this cypress-covered rock (middle distance), now inhabited by a hermit who lives on alms. This islet, called Pondikonisi, is thought by some to be the rock upon which Ulysses was cast by the tempest, and by others to be the Phaeacian vessel which was turned to stone when it returned to port after taking Ulysses to Ithaca. In the foreground is the monastery of the Blachernes, linked to Corfu by a jetty.

Tower of Belém, Lisbon, Portugal.

Nurtured on Islam and maritime discoveries across the Atlantic, the Portuguese Manueline style is displayed in a whole series of masterpieces, of which the Tower of Belém, or the Torre São Vicente, with its naturalistic rope moldings so alien in their decorative exuberance to the austere spirit of Chartres or Amiens, marks the apotheosis. Built between 1515 and 1521 in the middle of the Tagus on a fortified and casemated terreplein, the tower was gradually brought nearer the shore by alluvial deposits. The North African travels of its architect, Francisco d'Arruda, are no doubt responsible for some of its Moorish elements, notably the ribbed cupolas and the fantastic tower decorated with mullioned windows.

Driven by history,

the sons of the conquerors...

Pride in a hard-won daily victory can be seen in the haughty lines of the Portuguese fishing boats. Fishing off the Portuguese shores is still a life replete with peril and hardship. At the risk of their lives, the fishermen, stripped to the waist and bent over their oars like the galley slaves of old, cross the bar each day, winter and summer alike, to go a few miles out and net the sardines which provide their livelihood.

Portuguese "fragatas."   ▶

Nazaré, Portugal.

Algae harvest, Portugal.

Village famed for its miraculous catches of swordfish as well as sardines, Nazaré, on the coast of Portugal 140 miles from Lisbon, proudly displays its blue fishing boats hauled from the sea by oxen that wade in breast-deep. The ocean, which here takes on a Mediterranean blue, the whitewashed houses, the sand, the bright colors of the fishermen's clothes, contrast sharply with the black capes of the women who come and squat on the beach to await the return of the fishing fleet.

...continue their struggle with the implacable sea...

As though bearing a cross, the "sargaceiros" (seaweed gatherers) of Portugal shoulder the loads of nourishing algae which they wrest from the sea to use as fertilizer. Here at Costa Nova men and women wade out into the ocean and by dint of great effort harvest this marine fertilizer, which is indispensable for the cultivation of their little fields. These fields, scattered among channels and rice paddies, retain something of the texture of seaweed, and give a rather unusual look to the countryside.

◀ Breton fisherman, France.

Pointe du Raz, France.

...their faces are stony and stubborn...

This old sea dog, whose features seem to have been etched by the vastness of the ocean, reminds one of the hero of Ernest Hemingway's "The Old Man and the Sea." Too old to go to sea each day, this fisherman from Saint-Quay in Brittany cannot abandon the limitless horizons that have always exerted their fascination over sailors.

Figurehead of the old world, Pointe du Raz, this "little cape," as poet Paul Valéry called it, is the last salient of continental Europe, reaching out toward the New World. The jagged indentations of the Brittany coast are the result of the sea's harsh transgression. On the horizon, like a hairline, can be seen the Island of Sein.

41

Isle of Ushant, France.

Chausey Islands, France. ▶

...their blood beats to storm and tide...

Foaming tumultuously, angry ocean waves shatter on the jagged reefs of Ushant. Unpredictable and violent storms and currents on this part of the coast, together with dangerous reefs and heavy fogs, make the sea around the island especially hazardous. On December 10, 1791, the ship bringing the French writer François-René de Chateaubriand back from America almost foundered there. Ushant's frightening reputation is symbolized in a Breton proverb: "He who sights Belle-Ile sees his island; he who sights Croix sees his happiness; he who sights Ushant sees his blood." The lighthouse of Créac'h, a black and white striped tower rising some 200 feet above sea level, was first lit in 1862. Today it is equipped with one of the most powerful lamps in the world, and its beam can be seen 125 miles away.

Subject to the greatest tides in all Europe, most of the surface of the Chausey Islands lies visible only at the equinoxes. In six hours the sea level can fall forty-five feet, uncovering several square miles of sand and granite rocks, to which cling "long brown plants intertwined like hair." The earth then dries and puffs up in tiny scattered hummocks of sand which resemble nothing so much as gold nuggets.

Fishing boats off Brittany, France.

...calm or turbulent,

their sails rebuke the winds...

Conquerors of the wind, today's Sunday seafarers have rediscovered the sail, with the aid of which Europe's great legendary adventurers undertook their historic voyages of exploration. For some years now, thanks to various new easily handled models, the latest development in the nautical world, sailing is no longer restricted to experienced yachtsmen. In Europe as everywhere else, those who prefer solitude to the overcrowded beaches can now enjoy the pleasures of the open sea without having to be numbered among the wealthy.

Banners of the faith still fly high over Brittany, and the "pardon" is one of its most ancient manifestations. Each year crowds of pilgrims arrive to follow the processions, gather around chapels and calvaries, and present their offerings. On these occasions people still wear the traditional local costume. The most admired "pardons" are those of Finistère, but the most famous one takes place at Sainte-Anne-d'Auray, in Morbihan.

Breton "pardon," France.   ▶

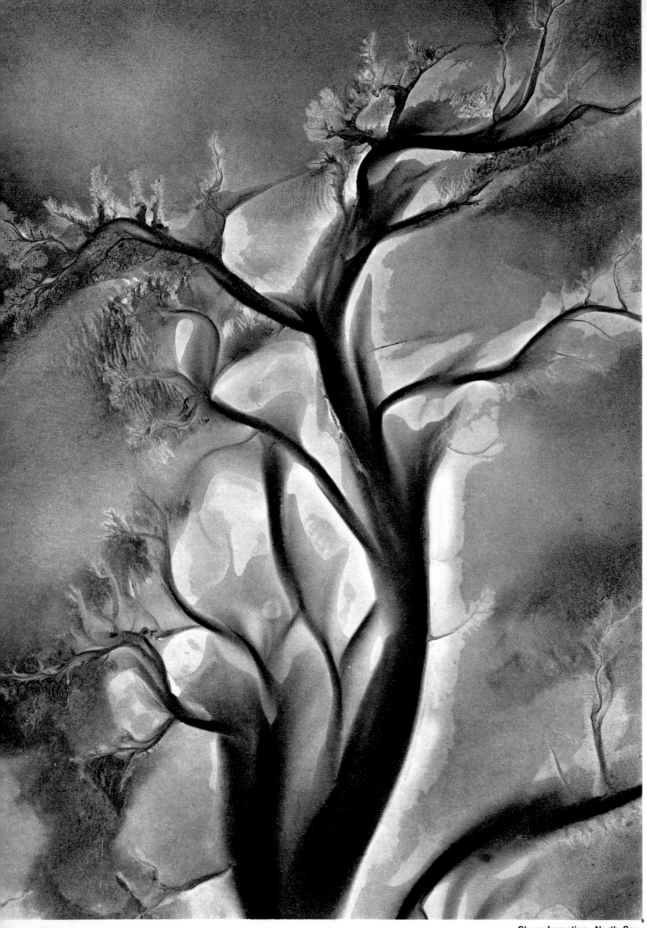

Shore formation, North Sea.

...their anguish

sharpens at the

sound of bells...

This weird-looking tree has been created by the ocean working on the sandy shores of the North Sea. The tides ebb and flow along a sinuous system of channels which has slowly been carved from the land. Vegetable-like forms are drawn in the sand and mud, resulting in those ill-defined stretches that the Germans call "Wattenmeer," literally "cotton-wool sea." A similar wasteland shaped by the waves, the bay of Mont-Saint-Michel spreads its vast beaches over fourteen square miles of sand and mud.

On the summit of Mont Tombe, so called because of its tomblike shape, Aubert, Bishop of Avranches, received from the Archangel Michael, who appeared to him in a dream, the order to erect a building in his honor. Sanctuary and citadel are inseparable. The ramparts and towers surround, like a suit of armor, the ancient buildings, set one on top of the other and topped by the soaring abbey church. "Here," exclaimed Victor Hugo, "one should pile up admiring superlatives just as men have piled buildings on the rocks." A Carolingian abbey supports a Romanesque abbey which is itself the sub-foundation for a Gothic abbey, giving Mont-Saint-Michel, in the words of De Maupassant, the look of a "monstrous jewel, as big as a mountain, carved like a cameo and as ethereal as silk muslin...."

Mont-Saint-Michel, France. ▶

Fisherman, St. Mary's Port, England.

Hardy descendant of a renowned people, this St. Mary's fisherman has the dark hair and complexion of his Celtic ancestors who took possession of the island in the ninth century B.C. St. Mary's, St. Martin's, Tresco, Bryher and St. Agnes are the only inhabited islands (with some 1,800 people) in the Scilly Isles, which comprise another 145 deserted islands. The archipelago was one of the last regions of the British Isles to be taken over by the Saxons, and popular speech still boasts expressions from Cornish, the old Celtic tongue spoken all over Cornwall until well after the end of the eighteenth century.

...but peace surges back

into the heart of the fisherman

who glimpses...

The desolate and peaceful Cornish coast still calls to mind the legendary battles which King Arthur and his Knights of the Round Table fought here more than thirteen centuries ago. Cornwall, with its huge rocks and its jagged coastline, is one of the most picturesque parts of the British Isles. These moorlands, sparsely covered by a variety of heather called "Erica vagans," gave birth to the old saying: "In Cornwall hardly enough wood grows to make a coffin."

◀ Cornwall, England.

... through coastal gateways, the fascination of the open sea.

Praia da Rocha, Portugal.

Cutting into the coastal rocks like a jigsaw, the sea has created all sorts of fantastic ornaments along Europe's Atlantic coast. The so-called Aiguille d'Etretat rises 200 feet out of the water, and is one of the landmarks of the Normandy coast. Viciously attacked at its base by waves carrying masses of pebbles, the cliff collapsed piece by piece, leaving behind a vertical wall on which the horizontal strata of which it is composed are clearly visible. Etretat's bold shapes, as well as the soft, veiled quality of the light that bathes these shores, furnished inspiration to many painters, especially Gustave Courbet and the Impressionists. Another example of the workings of the sea, Praia da Rocha, which lies some twelve miles north of Lisbon, literally bristles with reefs, the proud remnants of a promontory that was once an extension of the old mountains of Portuguese Estremadura. Differing considerably in their composition, the rocks offer unequal resistance to the waves. The softer rocks crumble, leaving the harder masses to form pillars and jut natural arches above the sea.

51

Sculptured by the elements, the northern shoreline...

Best-known and most romanticized of the "basalt organs" is the Giant's Causeway in Ireland, which was originally created by a volcano. A stream of lava cooled into thousands of almost parallel hexagonal or pentagonal shafts which are tinted in shades of red and yellow and arranged in three series. In all, there are 40,000 pillars.

Sculptured by tide and tempest, the cliffs of Old Harry Rocks, in Dorset on the southwest coast of England, are hollowed out into stalls, thrust forward in redans, and isolated in needles and pillars which are themselves threatened by erosion. For centuries this rocky labyrinth was the untroubled haunt of smugglers.

Giant's Causeway, Ireland.

Old Harry Rocks, England. ▶

Canal in the Netherlands.

A silver ribbon of water in which trees stripped bare by winter balefully gaze at their own reflections, the canal is an integral part of the Dutch scene. A network of over 3,000 miles of canals covers Holland. There is considerable activity on their waters; barges and lighters carry some 60 percent of the country's freight. It has been said that water offers that which is best and that which is worst in Holland. Without continual protection two-thirds of the country would be in constant danger of being flooded by tides, storms and swollen rivers. But throughout history, water has also served to arrest or slow the advance of would-be invaders, whether Spanish, French or German.

...offers magnificent

sweeps of nature...

The black masts of deserted boats form geometric patterns on a sea of ice as the skaters of Volendam, reminiscent of those of Brueghel's painting, dart toward the momentarily quiescent sea. With the first ice of the year, skating becomes a rite shared by people of all ages and walks of life. Competitions are organized, the most famous of which is the "Eleven Towns Race." It is held over a 125-mile course, and the winner is hailed all over Holland as a national hero.

Skaters in the Netherlands.   ▶

Scottish girl.

...where the mystery of life reflects the fantasy of the landscape...

Her face freckled, her hair windblown, her expression mischievous, nurtured on sea air, porridge and old legends, this girl symbolizes the soul of Scotland.   She knows a thousand and one tales of fairies and giants who roam the moors at night. But does she believe them or does she pretend to believe?   The Highland mind is perhaps the most impenetrable in the world.

In countryside bordering on the fantastic this solitary loch, from which a few rocks emerge like monsters from a bygone age, seems forever locked in an air of tragic melancholy.   Land of mists, chiaroscuro, mirages and phantasmagoria, the Scottish Highlands are truly disconcerting to the stranger.   Let a ray of sunlight break through the swiftly moving masses of clouds, and the seemingly eternal grayness will abruptly change into a precious stone as iridescent as an opal.   The mountain slopes are then decked out in brilliant colors ; emerald for the ferns, gold and mauve for the heather, silver for the waters of the loch.

Scottish loch.   ▶

Dyrholaey, the gateway to Iceland, known today as Cape Portland, served as a landmark for the Vikings. When the dragon figureheads of their longships passed the cape, they knew they were safely home. Lying 500 miles from the coast of Scotland, Iceland consists of nearly 40,000 square miles of lava, glaciers, rocky wastes and active volcanoes. Irish monks, coming to the island in the eighth century, described it as the underground forge of satanic blacksmiths. Today, boiling water still gushes from its crevasses, and is used to heat its houses and greenhouses.

Cape Portland, Iceland.

Kalmar Castle, Sweden.

Swedish bastion on the Baltic, Kalmar Castle was built by King Knut Erikson in the twelfth century. The Kalmar Union, under which the three Scandinavian countries were for 100 years united under the same crown, was proclaimed here in 1397. The history of all of Sweden turned on this hinge of stone until the final separation of the kingdoms of Norway and Denmark on the one hand and Sweden on the other. The ancient citadel crouching on the water perpetuates for the Swedes, so peaceful today, the memory of a glorious, warring past.

...or enhanced

by the silent glitter

of lofty peaks...

Gigantic offshore rocks, the melancholy Lofoten Islands raise their jagged shapes off Narvik, 100 miles north of the Arctic Circle. Branching fjords festoon and cut into the land, accentuating its rough, uneven character. But these harsh mountains hide valleys covered with rich grass and dotted with flowers. Despite the nearby presence of the fearsome strait of Maelstrom, the catch of fish, the archipelago's sole resource, is magnificent. Herring and cod abound, and can be seen drying everywhere, spread out on roofs or hung on lines like the weekly wash. In season, the little port of Reine can barely accommodate all the fishermen who swarm to the Lofotens. The Church has given them a dispensation to permit their working on the Sabbath, but the insurance companies insist that they land and rest one day a week after six consecutive days and nights of working their nets. In 1880 Reine was the scene of a desperate struggle between steamboats and sailboats. The trawlers managed to drive such a quantity of cod into this fjord that 9,500,000 were landed in a single week, a feat that was not to the liking of the fishermen in sailing boats, who reached the scene too late.

◀ Reine, Lofoten Islands, Norway.

...ranging

from the everyday

primitive...

The windswept dunes of Fan, an island off the west coast of Denmark, are hardly distinguishable from the billows of the North Sea. For centuries, all along these thirty miles of sandy coast, men have put to sea to fish for flounder, plaice and herring. Their wives and children wait, looking out to sea, the source of their joys and also of their sorrows.

Island of Fan, Denmark.   ▶

North Cape, Norway.

...to a black sun glowing on an icy sea.

Plunging sheerly almost 1,000 feet down into the water of the Arctic Ocean, North Cape, at the tip of Mageroy Island, is the closest point on the European continent to the North Pole. For four unending months the polar night veils these mountains of Pre-Cambrian schists, and for another four months the sun never sets on these northern lands. Louis-Philippe, when he was king of France, encouraged several expeditions to the North Cape between 1838 and 1843, notably those of the famed explorer Admiral Dumont d'Urville.

A dead volcano, its crater buried under a shroud of snow, Beerenberg rises to a height of 7,000 feet. The tiny island of Jan Mayen on which it stands lies far out in the Arctic Ocean on the edges of the ice pack whose floes block its shores each spring. The ocean has worked at the base of the mountain, leaving sharp cliffs and revealing the lava underneath. Since 1920 there has been a weather station on this inhospitable land, where summer is relatively colder than winter.

Beerenberg, Jan Mayen Island.　　　　　　　　　▶

THE MOUNTAINS

Rising majestically

at the heart

of the continent...

A mysterious bond unites the peaks of the Matterhorn and the mists that enfold them at day's end. The highest point of the Pennine Alps, between Swiss Valais and Italian Piedmont, the Matterhorn, or Mont Cervin, is a rocky pyramid 14,713 feet high. Its summit, conquered for the first time in 1865, dominates the valley of Zermatt, which itself is at an altitude of some 4,900 feet, and is the traditional starting point for Alpine climbing enthusiasts.

The Matterhorn, Switzerland. ▶

the dazzling

Alpine range,

with its ageless

fauna...

Majestic dome of Europe, the mighty bulk of Mont Blanc dominates Savoy, that most mountainous of French provinces, whose average altitude is 4,000 feet. A vast synclinal of crystalline schists, it is a young mountain rising to 15,781 feet. Only hunters in pursuit of chamois and rock collectors looking for crystals roamed its foothills when in 1760 a Geneva physician, Saussure, offered a generous prize to the first person to climb the mountain. Attempts began five years later, but the colossus was not conquered until 1786. The first men to reach the top were also from Geneva: Jacques Balmat and Dr. Paccard. Since then, successful climbs have been fairly frequent, but so have the accidents that have checkered the mountain's history.

◀ Mont Blanc, France.

Paradise for the almost extinct ibex, baroque embellishments of a solemn landscape, the Gran Paradiso in Italy is a worthy retreat for such handsome animals. Noteworthy for its flora and the variety of its Alpine scenery, the park—which also shelters herds of chamois—is a few miles from the Swiss frontier near Aosta, surrounded by a vast amphitheater of high mountains and glaciers.

Ibexes on the Gran Paradiso, Italy. ▶

...unrolls like a prodigious cyclorama.

Bernese Alps, Switzerland.

Like so many sleeping giants, the principal peaks of the Bernese Alps stretch across the horizon: the Jungfrau (13,653 feet), the Mönch (13,468 feet) and the Eiger (13,036 feet). The Bernese Alps are one of the Swiss ranges which, joined at the Saint Gotthard Pass, cover more than half the country. Its slopes boast one of the highest villages in Europe: Mürren, which at 5,415 feet hangs some 2,900 feet above the Lauterbrunnen valley. This group of mountains, with its high ski trails, its skating rinks and the longest cable-car run in Europe, the Firstbahn (at Grindelwald), is a paradise for the true lover of winter sports. Nine valleys, and an entire constellation of small Alpine lakes enliven the region where Byron wrote his well-known "Manfred" in 1816, taking a local legend as his inspiration.

Lake of Lucerne, Switzerland.

Lanoux Dam, French Pyrenees. ▶

An elegant technology

is overshadowed

by the glitter...

Standing in the snow, the sharp outlines of fir trees, looking as if they were etched by the hands of a Dürer, accentuate the shores of Lake Lucerne. This is the heart of historical Switzerland, where William Tell performed his famous feat of splitting the apple on his son's head with an arrow. It is the cradle of the Swiss Confederation. Over 700 feet deep, the lake is fed by the Reuss as it flows through the cantons of Uri, Unterwalden, Schwyz and Lucerne.

In the wild heart of the French Pyrenees, man has made his mark in attempting to harness the energy of the mountains. Lake Lanoux, the largest in the range, has been penned up by a 145-foot-high dam on the upper reaches of the River Carol, a tributary of the Ariège, not far from the frontier with Andorra. The reservoir thus created, 7,200 feet above sea level, helps to supply the power station at L'Hospitalet, which consists of three groups of generators capable of providing some 33,000 kilowatts of power.

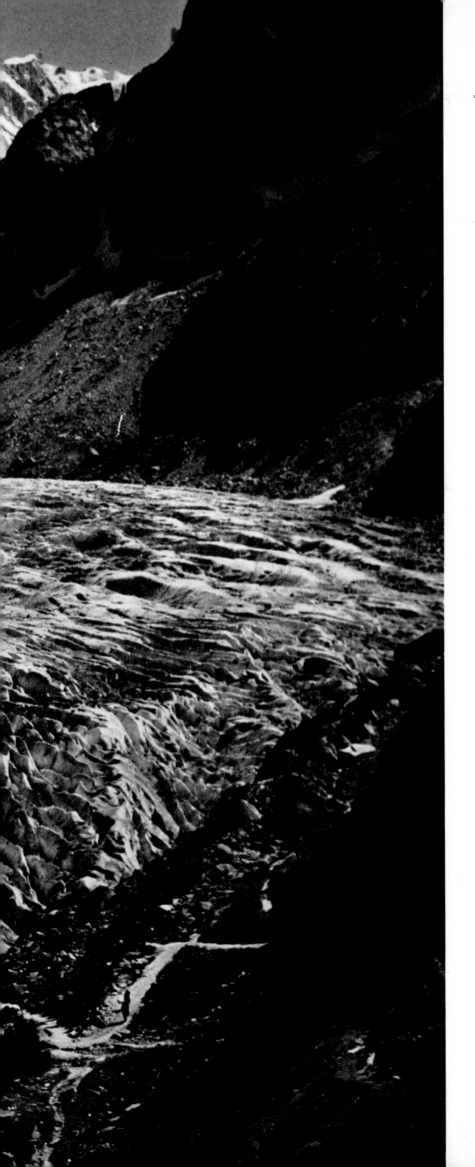

...of dizzying and ageless

glaciers...

Waves of eternal snow give the Mer de Glace the churned-up look of land under the plow.   It is the modest heir of the great glaciers that covered virtually all the northern Alps and the Durance Valley as far as Sisteron, some 20,000 years ago.   The Mer de Glace is three and a half miles long, averages 2,300 feet in width and is 930 feet thick. An inexorable mass, it advances about a foot a day, but is at the same time shrinking some twenty feet a year, gradually reducing the importance of the phenomenon of glacial erosion, which has been replaced today, in the southern Alps, by torrential erosion.

The Mer de Glace, Mont Blanc Range, France.

Monastery of La Grande Chartreuse, France.

The Dolomites, Italy. ▶

...sentinels at the abyss, like monks of an ancient order...

Sown like teeth on a cushion of green, the buildings of the Monastery of La Grande Chartreuse, not far from Chambéry, spread over twelve acres in the center of a large sloping meadow. St. Bruno was captivated by the peace and solitude of the spot when he decided, in 1084, to found the famed Carthusian Order. The bluish shadows of the firs add a warm note to this austere landscape, enclosed in a circle of steep cliffs. The monastery, the principal one of the Order, has been rebuilt several times.

The mauve outlines of the Dolomites rise over Italian Venetia. Bordered on the west by the Isarco and Adige valleys, on the north by the Rienza, and on the south by the Brenta and the Piave, they form part of the Italian Alps. Their color, varying from violet to bright red according to the strength of the sun's rays, is due to the predominance of dolomite—a natural carbonate of calcium and magnesium studied in 1795 by the mineralogist Dolomieu—in their geological constitution.

Aiguille du Roc, Mont Blanc range, France.

...beneath the eternal silence of the peaks.

A worthy adversary for the men who seek to measure their prowess against the severest challenges offered by the earth's mountains, this topmost monolith of the Aiguille du Roc is part of one of the Mont Blanc ranges. In order to climb it, a mountaineer must possess exceptional qualifications—only after overcoming enormous difficulties can one stand on its pinnacle, 11,181 feet high—and its conquest represents the ultimate in human capability. It is part of the Chamonix group of peaks which, rising above the town to the southwest, lie between the valley and the Glacier du Géant.

The German philosopher Nietzsche found inspiration as he looked on these scenes in the beautiful Engadine valley, where he twice came to rest and recuperate from illnesses. Here, in 1881, he had his famous vision of the "eternal recurrence" so central to all his philosophy; here too he drafted the second half of "Thus Spake Zarathustra." The Roseg valley, shown here, is part of the Bernina range which, lying on the borders of Switzerland, Austria and Italy, houses the magnificent Swiss national park.

◀ Bernina range, Switzerland.

Women of Evolène, Switzerland.

Hay barns, Valais, Switzerland. ▶

The persistent traditions of the people of the mountainsides...

Passionately devoted to the traditions of the past, the people of Valais are just as passionately attached to their land, for which they must wage an unceasing struggle against the mountain. Modern life seems to have changed nothing in the little villages of the canton of Valais. At Evolène, the women still wear their picturesque costumes, consisting of a simple dress with puffed sleeves, a brightly colored apron and a plaited-straw hat with the brim coming down slightly over the ears and the crown wound quaintly about with ribbons.

Gripping the mountain's flanks, Valaisan hay barns, or mazots, are built on piles topped by stone disks to keep out rodents. The farmers store their hay here, and even sleep here during the haying season. For in Switzerland going to the fields is almost like mountaineering. It is not possible to reach the fields by cart, nor can one return home at nightfall. The workers must stay on the spot for as long as the work lasts. Stored in these barns, the grass is left to dry, and when winter comes, is brought down to the farms on sledges.

Seefeld, Austria.

...transfigure the legendary

beauty of places...

Holy way station on the road to the peaks, the Seekapelle, at an altitude of 3,874 feet, is the parish church of the sports resort of Seefeld, in southwestern Austria. It was built in 1628 to house a miraculous cross, and contains three rococo altars. From Seefeld excursions are organized to the Reitherspitze, 7,100 feet high.

The baroque bell tower of the Church of St. Koloman injects a cheerful Eastern element in the romantic setting of the Bavarian forest. King Ludwig II chose this isolated site to build a dwelling place where he could dream of the fascinating medieval heroes of "Tannhäuser" or "Lohengrin," celebrated by his friend Wagner. This was the never finished Castle of Neuschwanstein—at left—built on the sheer Bertzenkopf rock, 3,165 feet above sea level. "The spot is one of the most beautiful places you could imagine," wrote the king to the composer. "It is sacred and inaccessible." The castle—which, according to the king's wishes, was without symmetry—was begun in 1869 on plans drawn up by a theatrical designer, Jank. It was in this retreat, in the heart of one of the best-loved regions of the Alps, that in 1886 the unfortunate monarch learned of his impending internment.

◀ Church of St. Koloman and Castle of Neuschwanstein, Germany.

Castle of Montebello, Bellinzona, Switzerland.

Lake Como, Italy. ▶

...where the epic past lingers.

A mailed fist in the laughing plain of Magadino, the citadel town of Bellinzona guards the roads to Italy followed by soldiers and merchants for centuries. The seat of the government of the only Italian-speaking Swiss canton, Ticino, it ranks among the smallest world capitals. Its charm, which held Ruskin there for the summer of 1858, is in good part due to the three medieval castles which, from their perches atop high rocky peaks, dominate it completely. The Castle of Montebello is a military construction built from the twelfth to the fifteenth centuries.

A fantasy setting, the lake valley is surrounded by the Alps. On Lake Como, called Larius by the Romans, between Colico and Lecco, opposite the little island of Comacina, stands the Church of Santa Maria Maddalena, surrounded by terraced gardens on the hillsides and rows of trees which grow right down to the water's edge. Its eleventh century Lombardic belfry with its double windows is the oldest monument on the shores of Lake Como, the home of the industrious masons who created the famous Lombardic style.

Saint Gotthard Road, Switzerland.

Grand Canyon of the River Verdon, France. ▶

The most

dizzying

access roads...

An elegant necklace adorning the approaches to the Saint Gotthard Pass, the road linking the Swiss and Italian lakes is one of the most beautiful in Switzerland. In Ticino it crosses the Saint Gotthard Pass, the top of which, at an altitude of 6,929 feet, is a desolate rock-strewn plateau. The mountain range, called Adula by the ancients, owes its name to a famous hermit who lived in the Alps.

A twisted scar gashed into the rock, the Grand Canyon of the Verdon is one of the wildest spots in Europe. At the heart of a vast Jurassic formation of white limestone some thirteen miles long—from Rougon to the bridge of Aiguines—the river has carved out a series of gorges through which the water gushes at a speed of six feet per second. Into this fearful cleft—at times 2,296 feet deep—surge the waters of the Verdon from the east, the torrential waters of the Baou from the west, and, lower down, the waters of the Artuby. It was not until 1905 that it was navigated for the first time, with the help of collapsible boats. Several years ago the place was judged suitable for the construction of a dam, but two successive projects had to be abandoned because of the excessive fissuring that occurred in the rocky walls of the reservoir while the dam was being built.

...studded with remarkable rock formations...

Like fingers pointing skyward, chimneys, or "fairy pyramids," raise their elegant silhouettes in the country around Théus. A frequent phenomenon in the morainic soil of the Alps, the formation of these curiously topped structures takes place gradually. Blocks of stone, generally carried far from their original surroundings by glacial ice, come to rest on softer ground which they then tend to protect from erosion. As the rains slowly wash away the surrounding soil, the peak gradually emerges.

◀ Ravine of Théus, France.

Crowned with glaciated sandstone, the peaks of Montserrat to the northwest of Barcelona reign over the Catalonian countryside. Like the surrounding terrain, the mountain range is composed of sandstone rocks which owe their dark red color to the presence of iron oxide. They contain fossils from the warm seas of the Jurassic period. Only a few narrow and difficult passages lend access to the heights. This site, endowed with excellent natural protection, was chosen in the ninth century by Benedictine monks to build a monastery.

Montserrat, Spain. ▶

...end in a spectacular assault on the very heavens.

San Clemente de Tahull, Spain.

...the fierce conquerors of the mountains...

Built to defy time, the tiny Church of San Clemente de Tahull is an excellent example of that robust Romanesque architecture which blends so harmoniously with the Spanish Pyrenees. Consecrated in 1123, the same year as the Church of Santa Maria in the same hamlet of Tahull, its interior was adorned with fine polychrome revêtements of which the paintings from the central apse and one of the smaller apses are now preserved in the Museum of Ancient Art in Barcelona. Five stories high, the square tower next to the church was a departure from the usual style of Lombardic towers in the eleventh century. Its shape and red ochre color are closer to Italian towers.

Citadel of the faith, standing firm on the arid slopes of the Sierra de las Rosas in Spain, the Benedictine monastery of San Pedro de Roda, still often referred to as San Cristobal, the name of a neighboring peak, was built in the Romanesque Byzantine style. The surrounding mountains are a part of the Pyrenees, which in the northeast of the peninsula determine the topography of the Costa Brava (literally "wild coast") with its magnificent rugged scenery.

San Pedro de Roda, Spain.   ▶

Puy de Pariou, France.

...have dotted the volcanic masses

A rosary of craters, the mountains of the Puy (peak) district of Auvergne seem to have been set on the plateau by mere whim. The Puy de Pariou is composed of volcanic materials—pumice, grit, round stones, scoria, granite—which seem to have just been ejected from an active crater. The crater of the Puy de Pariou has a circumference of 3,116 feet and a depth of 315 feet. Cows graze in its spacious bowl.

Sainte-Foy, France.

with masterpieces...

A sacred plant nestling in a valley of the Aveyron "département," the Church of Sainte-Foy looks out reassuringly over the old town of Conques, formerly the site of one of the richest monasteries in France. The church, begun between 1041 and 1052 by Abbot Odobric, was finished at the beginning of the twelfth century. Its architecture was doubtless a source of inspiration for many Romanesque churches in Auvergne. In the fourteenth century Sainte-Foy, until then a popular stopping place on the pilgrim road to Santiago de Compostela, went into a decline. Converted to secular uses in 1424, it was damaged in 1568 by a fire started by Protestant fanatics. Abandoned during the Revolution, it was rediscovered in 1837 by the writer Prosper Mérimée who was at that time inspector general of historical monuments. Restorative work was carried on throughout the nineteenth century and a museum was built to house its ancient collection of relics and ornaments, the most important bequeathed to us from the Middle Ages.

Vosges, France.

Haut-Koenigsbourg, France. ▶

...whose turrets overhang the nearby lakes...

Peaceful lakeside slopes, the wooded hills of the Vosges stretch like great crouching animals. The countryside, in this land of gentle mounds, at its highest reaches only 4,672 feet. Its hills were shaped by the action of the Moselle glacier which broke up to form the tributary valleys of the Saône and left typical glacial sites: striated glaciated rocks alternating with lakes enclosed by moraines reaching 260 feet in height.

An impregnable eyrie, surrounded by three fortified walls on a sharp and solitary peak in the Vosges, the Castle of Haut-Koenigsbourg, built from red sandstone, overlooks the entire plain of Alsace. In 1480 it was rebuilt by Count Oswald of Thierstein. In 1648 the Treaty of Westphalia gave it to France, but it was abandoned for more than 200 years before being taken over and restored by Kaiser Wilhelm II.

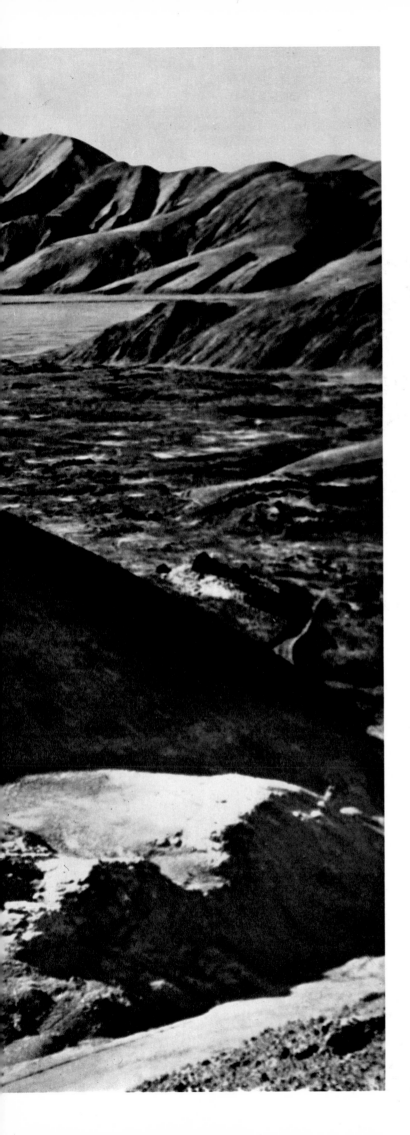

Mount Saksa, Norway.

...mirrors to marvelous sublunar landscapes.

Its snow-flecked crest reflected in the clear waters of Sogne Fjord, Mount Saksa is one of the dominant features of one of the oldest lands in the world—Norway. A quarter of the country is covered by forests, two-thirds of it is absolutely barren, and it is rich in fjords. Sogne Fjord is the longest and most important of these, with a depth of 350 fathoms in some places. The landscape along its 112-mile length is sometimes harsh, sometimes smiling.

The lunar landscape of southern Iceland seems to have been devastated long before the birth of man. Landmannalaugar is the volcanic region par excellence of this largest island in Europe. Springs and geysers are everywhere, and favor the cultivation of flowers and market gardens. The "land of ice" boasts Europe's largest glacier, Vatnajökull, which covers some 3,300 square miles and reaches an altitude of 6,952 feet.

◀ Landmannalaugar, Iceland.

Monk, Meteora, Greece.

Dazzled by the preternatural aspect of the mountaintops...

This man of God chose solitude, following the monastic tradition that brought the first monks here 600 years ago. The Meteora was created between 1356 and 1372 by the monk Athanasius. He imposed a strict code of living upon the nine monks who lived with him; no woman was to enter the monastery or receive food there. In the sixteenth century the Orthodox monasteries declined after corruption had become rife. From twenty-four their number shrank to four, among whom a few monks of the Order of St. Basil have been scattered through the years.

The desolate shapes of the Meteora stand in a remote corner of Thessaly. Here and there monasteries with overhanging roofs and wooden balconies jut out. In former times there were no roads leading to the monasteries and visitors could enter only by means of articulated ladders 50 to 100 feet high, which were drawn up at the first sign of danger. Another means of gaining entry was by being hoisted up in a net, which today is only used to haul up provisions, since steps have been installed for human beings.

◀ Meteora, Greece.

The Temple of Apollo at Delphi, and Mount Kirphi, Greece.

Mount Olympus, Greece. ▶

...man has abandoned places haunted by dead gods...

The memory of mystic trances that seized the Pythia of Delphi here 2,000 years ago still haunts this enchanting spot where the ancient Greeks once came to consult their gods. With its springs, crevasses, and the strange effluvia which rise from the ground, the Oracle's setting is most impressive—which helps explain the religious role that Delphi has played from almost the very beginnings of history. The fame of the Oracle and of the magnificence of the Pythian feasts spread throughout the ancient world.

Realm of the gods is the jagged peak of Mount Olympus. Situated between Macedonia and Thessaly, it is the highest peak in Greece, rising 9,573 feet into the sky. Its most noticeable features—Skolion, 9,570 feet; the Throne of Zeus, 9,550 feet; Skala, 9,400 feet—are grouped in an amphitheater in the center of the range, surrounding the wild Mavrolongos valley. A sacred mountain covered with eternal snows, Olympus has given its name to several lesser Greek mountains.

Greek shepherd.

Greek shepherds, keepers of the wisdom of the centuries, still wander over a land sown with history and legend. They are the sole survivors of the pastoral and warlike civilizations that in bygone days flourished on these now desolate hills. In a country where 80 percent of the land is mountainous and the remainder is mainly pastureland, sheep-raising is still one of the chief resources, especially in Attica, the Peloponnesus and the islands.

Stark setting for tragedy, its mountains bearing the names of Erymanthos (formerly Olonos), Taygetus and Parnon: the Peloponnesus, or island of Pelops, is the southernmost part of Greece. According to legend, Pelops, son of Tantalus, was fed to the gods by his father during a banquet. He was brought back to life by Jupiter. Then, by means of a "rigged" chariot race, he won both the hand of Hippodamia and the peninsula that was to bear his name. Marbled with inlets, the Peloponnesus has kept to its traditional agriculture. It supplies grapes from Corinth, olives from Kalamata and fruit from Argos which have been famous since antiquity.

Peloponnesus, Greece.

...but pastoral life animates the bright slopes...

The White Horse, Great Britain.

...like shadows

on a sacred hillside.

A phantom from the past, the monumental white horse carved out of the chalk in the Berkshire landscape commemorates a defeat inflicted on the Danes by the English king Alfred the Great (848-899). From the earliest times, man has exploited to artistic ends the natural possibilities offered by the limestone hills in these regions. Several of these immense designs have survived, notably two giants, one in Dorset, the other in Worcestershire, which are thought to have been Saxon totems. Today, the periodic restorations of the figures are occasions for gay regional festivities.

A long snow-covered ridge, Mount Hekla rises 4,747 feet in the southwestern part of the volcanic island of Iceland. It is always active, as witness the steam which continually escapes from its crater, and to which it owes its name: ''hekla'' means ''mantle.'' It has erupted twenty-three times since the twelfth century, the most recent eruption, a spectacular one accompanied by an earthquake, having occurred on March 29, 1947; columns of smoke and ashes were visible fifteen miles away while wide streams of molten lava slithered down the volcano's sides. Mount Hekla, if it is not Iceland's most important volcano, is certainly its most famous.

◀ Mount Hekla, Iceland.

◄ The Roman bridge, Mostar, Yugoslavia.

Peasant women on the shores of Lake Ochrida, Yugoslavia.

The echoes of past poetry...

The daily life of Yugoslav peasant women is conditioned by an omnipresent nature. Modern civilization with all its scientific and mechanical techniques has not yet divorced them from the traditional ways in which their ancestors lived. These women, washing clothes on the shore of Lake Ochrida, can see in the distance the hills of ancient Lychnidos, called Akhrida by the Byzantines. Ruled over in turn by Greeks (fourth century B.C.), Romans, barbarians and Byzantines (from the sixth to the eleventh centuries), and joined to Hungary in the twelfth century, Yugoslavia, most of whose territory had been occupied by Italy, Turkey and Austria, was only born as an independent state in 1919, by the union of the southern Slavs with Serbia. It has nonetheless maintained a strong sense of its unity, as was proved by the heroic resistance the country put up during World War II.

Ensconced between two rocky ramparts 195 feet in height, the little Yugoslav town of Mostar, principal economic and cultural center of Herzegovina, straddles the Neretva, whose banks are joined by several bridges. One of these, the Roman bridge—seen in our photograph—dates from the days when the district was part of Tiberius' empire. But the original bridge survives in name only. Indeed, the present bridge was built between 1566 and 1567 by the great Turkish architect Hajrudin. Spanning the river with a single arch, 88 feet wide and 65 feet high, it is flanked at each end by massive towers.

◀ Folk dancing, Rumania.

Koprivshtitsa, Bulgaria.

...amplified by the surroundings and by rustic tradition...

Tucked away in the undulations of the Sredna Gora, Koprivshtitsa is one of the few Bulgarian towns which have managed to preserve their typical local architecture. No one knows when the town was founded. Still, five centuries of Turkish occupation were unable to suppress a craft whose exuberance can still be seen on old doorways, carved balconies and wooden-latticed windows. Squat and strong, half hidden by ivy and boxwood, the houses seem to have been cast from ever-changing molds.

Most exuberant of central and eastern European peoples, the Rumanians are also the only ones with Latin origins. One of the first to draw on their folklore was the Hungarian composer Béla Bartók. Several trips and the tenacity of a collector enabled him to gather from the very mouths of peasants pentatonic melodies so splendid that he used them as the bases of many of his works. The absolute ruler over rural life in years gone by, custom had established a regular code of songs and dances for all occasions in life: harvest, haymaking, the Feast of St. John, Easter and so on. . . . Marriages were celebrated according to very precise rites; there were dances and wedding songs for each phase in the actual ceremony as well as the long preparations leading up to it.

113

...hallow the daily life...

◀ Mykonos, Greece.

Mytilene, Greece.

Playing games and talking around a café table, in some quiet shaded little square, is as old as the Greek islands themselves. At Mytilene the people have kept to a traditional way of life which has been strongly influenced by the long Turkish occupation, which lasted from the end of the fifteenth century until 1912, despite attempts at liberation in 1464 and 1501. Once the home of the poets Alcaeus and Sappho, the ancient Lesbos is today a mountainous and volcanic land of over 100,000 inhabitants where old-fashioned weaving sheds still exist alongside a few modern industries such as soapworks, oilworks and tanneries.

Ample beacon of ancient Greek civilizations, this picturesque sail windmill is one of the finest on the hill of Kato Mili on Mykonos. The island, so the legend runs, was the piece of rock with which Poseidon annihilated the Giants. It is an island famed for the skill and courage of its seamen, who distinguished themselves from the beginning of the war of independence against the Turks, in 1821. Mykonos today, thanks to its natural beauty, the charm of its village, and its closeness to Delos, is the best known summer resort in the Cyclades.

...of southern

peasants

faithful

to their legend.

◀ Girl spinning, Crete, Greece.

Peribleptos Monastery, Mistra, Greece.

Rooted in the dry red earth, the monasteries at Mistra, in the Peloponnesus (above, the monastery of Peribleptos), constitute the most important collection of monuments that modern Greece owes to its Byzantine heritage. As the central power decayed on the Bosporus, provincial administrators became more and more important and caused countless buildings of a religious nature to be erected as evidence of their autonomy. Mistra owes its splendor to this period. The town was born in the thirteenth century, below a protecting fortress built by the Crusader Guillaume de Villehardouin. Byzantine Emperor Michael Palaeologus seized it around the year 1265, and until 1460 Mistra was, although under the authority of governors who became more and more independent, the wealthy capital of the Byzantine Despotate of Morea. Afterward, through successive Turkish and Venetian occupations, it maintained its reputation as the "wonder of the Peloponnesus." Goethe was so impressed that he set the key scene of the second part of his "Faust," Faust's meeting with Helen, here.

Like Ariadne at the entrance to the labyrinth, anxiously awaiting the return of Theseus, the conqueror of the Minotaur, this graceful Cretan girl hugs her distaff of flax. Five thousand years ago, the extraordinary Minoan civilization flourished on this island. It was a key period in the history of art, lying midway between Egypt and Greece, and to it we owe the marvelous constructions at Phaestus and Knossos. A hardy and hospitable people live here today, lovers of dancing, especially the whirling "pentozali," which no foreigner has ever managed to imitate. They love singing too, especially the "mantinades," lyric couplets sung in chorus to the accompaniment of a "lyra."

The curious

and elegant

plan

of the villages...

The roofs of Alberobello, huddled like a crowd of small extinct volcanoes near Lecce in Apulia, remind us of the first villages that men built in the prehistoric forest glades when they ventured out of their caves. These "trulli," as they are called, are built by means of a technique which predates the discovery of mortar and timbering. First a circle is made of flat stones set side by side. Then a slightly smaller circle of stones is placed on top of the first circle, and so on until a height is reached at which the remaining hole at the top can be covered by a single stone. By omitting stones from a portion of each circle a door is made, and if one joins two "trulli" door to door, one has a house with two communicating rooms. The chimneys rising from the added façades are the only anachronism in Alberobello.

◀ Alberobello, Italy.

A geometric puzzle, the flat roofs of Skyros are speckled with clumps of earth that will be spread out in bad weather to protect the houses from the cold. It was on this island that Achilles was hidden by his mother, who sought to prevent his taking part in the siege of Troy for fear a lance thrust might pierce his vulnerable heel. Skyros is also the burial place of the British poet Rupert Brooke, who died of a fever during the Dardanelles campaign. The inhabitants of the island keep themselves busy during the winter by making household goods which are highly prized throughout Greece. Custom decrees that they should bring back from their travels plates to hang on their walls. Several houses on Skyros have thus become small museums of ancient and valuable earthenware.

Skyros, Greece. ▶

Siphnos, Greece.

Peasant women of the Peloponnesus, Greece. ▶

...the majesty

of towns built

around

a patriarchy...

A music score of white notes dotted on a tiered landscape, these houses, perfect cubes shining in the sun, can be found everywhere in the Cyclades, a group of islands so called because they form a circle around Delos. Siphnos, small, severe, and off the beaten track, is a dry, barren schistous dome where the earth is cultivated by intensive Mediterranean methods. Gardens and small farms are scrupulously maintained on its irrigated terraces. In ancient times the island was wealthy enough, thanks to the production of its gold mines, to deliver a magnificent treasure to the temple of Apollo at Delphi.

Descendants of the Spartans, once militarily the most powerful people in Greece, these washerwomen today fulfill their simple lot as housewives, in a setting still charged with epic grandeur. The Spartan plain, dominated by Mount Taygetus, gashed with crevasses and ravines, where a standing army of olive trees seems to salute the visitor, is today a rich agricultural valley producing a famed olive oil as well as a bountiful harvest of honey, lemons and oranges.

... the solemn splendor

of ruins

glorifying nature...

Stripped of its lava shroud, the dead city of Pompeii proudly exhibits to the tourist the exact planning with which its streets were laid out; it would be easy to imagine a group of toga-clad patricians pacing between the columns. Founded by the Oscans in the sixth century B.C., the city owes much of its appearance to its occupation by Samnites (425 to 420 B.C.). In 82 B.C. it was elevated to the rank of a full Roman colony, Colonia Veneria Cornelia Pompeii, and became a pleasure ground popular with the best families of Roman society. A hundred years later, its 20,000 inhabitants perished, buried beneath a layer of pumice stone that was subsequently covered by the ashes from Vesuvius. At the end of the sixteenth century, the architect Domenico Fontana discovered inscriptions which encouraged speculation that important ruins lay hereabouts. But it was not until 1748 that excavations began, bringing to light this immense tomb. Uninterrupted research from that day forward has enabled scholars to reconstruct almost perfectly the life of the ancient city. In the homes, household objects have been restored to their proper places, and on the walls many inscriptions written in red letters still remain intact. The Villa of the Mysteries, a vast triangular building dating from the third century B.C., holds various aspects of the buried city. The interplay of perspective and color creates an illusion of space in some of its rooms, which are decorated in the architectural style fashionable at the time. In the "room of the great painting," magnificent frescoes in soft pastel shades call to mind the religious world of the Romans that was dominated by the Orphic or Dionysiac mysteries. Pompeii is today one of the high spots of Italian archaeology.

◄ Pompeii, Italy.

Giant olive trees in Calabria, Italy.

...are the testament of a history

written in stone and bark.

"The tree of Pallas, long-lived Olive," sung by Virgil in his "Georgics," spreads its shade over the lands of the Mediterranean basin. Its silver-gray leaves sparkled in the Italian sun 2,000 years ago, just as they did in the "Odes" of Horace or the "Elegies" of Tibullus. Native to Asia Minor, the tree, which to the ancients was a symbol of peace, spread to Greece, Italy and Spain. The Phocaeans introduced it into France when they founded the city of Marseilles. The olive and the olive press are among the elements that have characterized the Mediterranean civilization.

A lone and haughty rampart of light-colored stone, the Castel del Monte stands on an isolated hill in the Murge overlooking the plain of Apulia. It was built about 1240 by Frederick II of Swabia who sought to erect both a fortress and a resting place for his hunting parties. Romano-Gothic in style, but built to a strict octagonal plan, the castle has eight 78-foot-high towers, one at each corner. The interior exhibits a striking, near-oriental comfort which was exceptional for its time. The arrangement of water mains and the latrines in each tower indicate that the emperor took his inspiration from castles in Syria built by the Crusaders, which he had visited during his stay in the Middle East.

◀ Castel del Monte, Italy.

125

Villa Pisani, Stra, Italy.

▸Country around San Gimignano, Italy. ▸

Palaces as stylized as landscapes...

A setting for princely festivities, the Villa Pisani, near Stra, is one of the most splendid to be seen in the Venetian states. Built when Alvise Pisani was elected Doge of Venice in 1735, it was intended to offer a suitable background for the pomp with which he surrounded himself. It can pride itself on having welcomed Napoleon, czars, emperors and Austrian archdukes, all of whom explored its famous maze, its wide avenues and its ballroom with a ceiling embellished with frescoes by Tiepolo.

"The cypresses believe in God." Their black silhouettes add a melancholy note to the beauty of the Tuscan countryside. Even for the ancients these trees expressed spirituality. Their noble lines, blending with the curves of the hills, are an ever-present element in the Tuscan scene. Traveling through this privileged corner of Italy, stretching from Pisa to Siena and taking in Florence and Arezzo, the visitor can readily understand the miracle of the first Renaissance, of Giotto and of Piero della Francesca.

...the admirable natural harmony that welcomes meditation...

Land of burning faith and fruitful meditation, Monte Oliveto Maggiore (23 miles southwest of Siena in Tuscany) houses a red brick monastery, the main establishment of the Olivetans, which lies hidden in a swell of cypress and olive trees. The monks stroll happily through the rough landscape to relax from the strain imposed by their studies. The Olivetans belong to the Congregation of the Order of St. Benedict which was founded in 1319 by Bernard Tolomei of Siena. The story of his life is told in the superb frescoes by Luca Signorelli and Sodoma which decorate the walls of this famous monastery.

◀ Monte Oliveto, Italy.

Broken witnesses to the glories of the Provincia Romana, these granite columns of a Roman temple lend the country around Riez, in the "département" of the Basses-Alpes, an elegance imbued with a somewhat nostalgic classicism. From the fifth to the eighteenth centuries the prosperous seat of a bishopric, the little town of Riez abounds in ruins that attest to its Gallo-Roman origins. It was indeed on the plateau at the foot of Mont Sainte-Maxime that the ancients chose to build the city of Reia on the River Collostre, not far from the magnificent gorge of the Verdon. For reasons of security, in the Middle Ages the city was gradually forced to invade the slopes and ultimately establish itself on the summit of the hill.

Riez, France. ▶

...the metaphysical

parallel

of time frozen

and time flowing...

In rugged sun-scorched mountains, the Temple of Segesta, in western Sicily, stands alone in the midst of an impressive silence broken only by occasional gusts of wind and the sound of sheep bells. It is a Doric edifice dating from 425 B.C. with a peristyle of thirty-six pillars without flutings. The builders started their work on the exterior of the temple. They departed, leaving it unfinished, about 409 B.C. Traditional in conception, this structure bears witness to the great technical skill of its builders. Preserved intact, the temple is the only remaining witness to ancient Segesta, the city of the Elymians; this city, in the fifth century a great rival to its flourishing neighbor Selinunte, sought aid in an alliance first with the Athenians then with the Carthaginians. The Vandals and the Saracens were to destroy it completely around the year 1000.

◄ Segesta, Sicily.

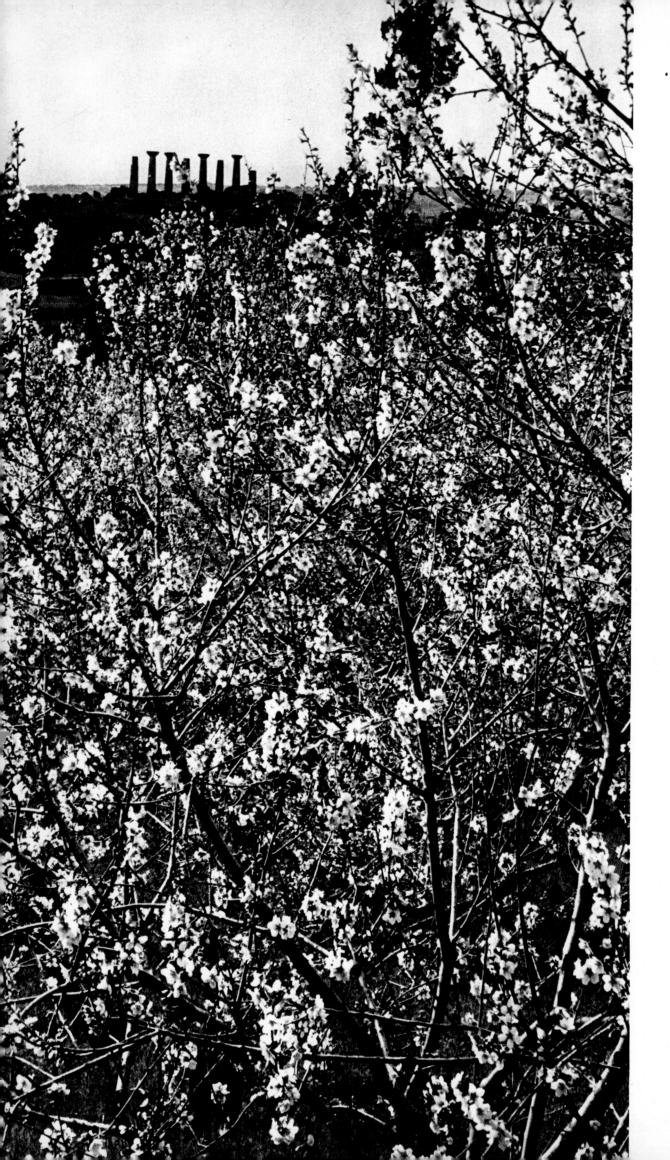

...the simultaneous burgeoning of springtime and the flowers of art...

Outpost of the Greek miracle, Agrigento spreads its panorama of almond trees and temples toward the facing African shore. Built on a hill, the ancient Akragas of the Greeks possesses—after Greece itself—the grandest collection of Doric monuments in the world, the remains of which are scattered along the Valley of the Temples. Founded in 581 B.C. by the inhabitants of Gela, a neighboring town, the birthplace of Empedocles and Pirandello passed into the hands of the Romans in 340 A.D., and was destroyed by the Saracens in 829. Next to the ancient ruins is the modern town with its 41,000 inhabitants.

◀ Agrigento, Sicily.

Flamboyant witness of an ephemeral harmony between the Norman and Siculo-Arabic styles, the cloister of Monreale (1174-1182), supported by 216 twin columns and surmounted by varyingly sculptured capitals, stands outside Palermo as if to recall that Sicily was, in the twelfth century, one of the great crossroads of European civilization. It was the Norman William II who founded the cloister and church of Monreale, the finest in Sicily. Following the example of the other Norman monarchs, who erected palaces which were inspired by Arabic styling, he invited Christians, Greeks and Moslems to work together, protected by the same laws, on the decoration of this masterpiece, which is also a monument to tolerance.

Monreale. The cloister, Sicily. ▶

◀ Villa Lante, Bagnaia, Italy.

Villa Garzoni, Collodi, Italy.

...the blooming genius of the landscape architect...

The rush of artificial waterfalls has given the Villa Lante, near Bagnaia, its reputation for possessing one of the most beautiful gardens in Italy. Begun in 1566 by Cardinal Gambera, Bishop of Viterbo, and completed by his successor, Cardinal Montalto, it later came into the possession of the Lante family, who gave it their name. The planner of the gardens, Vignola, sought (left) to imitate the course of a river, with all its irregularities. The waters of the Villa Lante bubble out from between two small summerhouses on a wooded hill and fall noisily from a waterfall shaped like a long crayfish (the animal represented on the coat of arms of the first cardinal). They then emerge peacefully into a wide stream in the middle of a slab of stone.

Designed as if for elegant parties, the gardens of the Villa Garzoni, at Collodi, owe their spectacular appeal to the ingenuity of an architect who was able to turn a difficult situation to his own profit. The gardens were begun in 1652 to adorn the medieval castle which the Garzoni family bought and transformed into a luxurious villa. The rather inconvenient site of the old dwelling, perched on a height above the village, made it necessary for the gardens to be set out on a lower level and to the side, with the result that the brilliant flower beds and the play of the fountains can be witnessed from the windows of the villa. At the end of the seventeenth century Ottaviano Diodati improved the machinery, adding a stage for an orchestra behind the uppermost terrace.

La Coste, France.

Pont du Gard, France.

Folk Festival, Arles, France.

...lend enchantment to the "tableaux vivants" of the southern countryside.

Sunburnt serenity bathes the little village of La Coste, which is overlooked by the massive fortress in which the famed Marquis de Sade lived for many years before his imprisonment. La Coste lies peacefully in the countryside of the Vaucluse "département," in the heart of Avignon. Sprawling between the Rhône and the purple hills of the Provençal Alps, it was originally a dry and unproductive basin. Now irrigated by channels from the picturesque and bubbling spring of the Vaucluse, the reddish-brown surface of the plain is spotted with the green of orchards and gardens.

Their delicate necks and sheer muslin combine to give the women of Arles their gentle and attractive air. If in Provence, as throughout the whole of present-day Europe, local costumes are gradually disappearing, the traditional dress of Arles is among those that is managing best to resist the trend—probably because it is the most beautiful dress of the region. It consists of a long skirt and an extremely tight-fitting bodice, worn half open at the front. "It is there, on the front of this well-filled bodice," wrote the French poet Frédéric Mistral, "that they display their jewels and gold ornaments to such an extent that this part of their costume is called the 'capello'—the 'chapel.'" The costume is completed by a headdress wound around with a velvet ribbon.

The three tiers of arches of the Pont du Gard, one of the masterpieces of Roman civil engineering, cross the valley toward Nîmes, their golden stones highlighting the natural harmony of the Provençal scene. Nine hundred and two feet long and 157 feet high, it was built by order of Agrippa, son-in-law of Augustus, about the year 19 B.C., to support the aqueduct carrying water to Nîmes from the neighborhood of Uzès.

Baked like the earth, the people...

Christmas at Les Baux, France.

Les Baux, France. ▶

"Fear not; for, behold, I bring you good tidings of great joy, which shall be to all people," declared the angel to the shepherds of Bethlehem 2,000 years ago. It is as a result of this utterance that once each year, as the Midnight Mass is being celebrated in the Church of Les Baux in Provence, the secular feast of the shepherds, the ''pastrage,'' also takes place. During the offertory, a priest hidden behind the altar announces the birth of Christ to the shepherds, as did the angel. The congregation then moves forward, preceded by pipes and tabors—the shepherds in their great cloaks, their wives in their shawls and wearing their ''garbalins,'' pointed bonnets decorated with lace and fruit. In their midst is a cart of painted wood, festooned with ribbons and candles and drawn by a ram; it bears a newborn lamb of which the prior and all the brotherhood after him make an offering. Regulated today by a liturgy that has been purged of its secular, and even pagan elements, the feast of the ''pastrage'' was frequently forbidden in past times.

A tragic fate seems to have befallen the ancient city of Les Baux, whose strange ruins cling to the top of a sheer cliff on the slopes of the Provencal Alps. Since the site is a natural defensive position, it has been inhabited from prehistoric times. After a period as a Roman colony, the town in the tenth century came under the sway, along with the entire lower Durance region, of a feudal family who took for their name that of the rock (Baou) on which they had built one of their castles. The house of Les Baux, claiming descent from King Balthazar, one of the Three Wise Men, took the Star of Bethlehem as its coat of arms. After enjoying great prosperity and a period as one of the centers of the refined civilization of the troubadours of the Middle Ages, the city was demolished in 1632 on the orders of Louis XIII as punishment for having supported the rebellion of Gaston d'Orléans, and was given to the princes of Monaco.

Castle of Almourol, Portugal.

Spanish woman spinning. ▶

...traditionally

come of age

in the shadow of

monuments...

Steeped in legend, the Castle of Almourol, standing majestically on an island on the Tagus, has excited the imagination of Portuguese storytellers for hundreds of years. It is one of the most curious specimens of twelfth-century military architecture existent. Built originally by the Romans, it was reconstructed in 1171 by Gualdim Pais, grand master of the Templars. All that now remains is the high keep or "tower of homage," and the enceinte, still intact with its ten turrets pierced by barbicans—long and narrow loopholes through which archers could shoot in safety—whose battlements were mostly rebuilt in the nineteenth century. The story goes that at the foot of the ruins, those who care to look into the clear waters of the Tagus below the vegetation-enshrouded ruins on moonlit nights can see the ghosts of a beautiful princess and a Moorish prisoner locked in each other's arms as they relive their forbidden love after so many centuries.

The charm of a centuries-old gesture is clearly apparent as this woman sits spinning yarn in her native southern Spain. Sentries of the past, old women throughout the whole of the Mediterranean basin serve as guardians of tradition and popular speech. It is they who pass on Christian legends and traditions which they color with a kind of primitive fervor. In the evenings, as they spin their flax by the light of oil lamps, they tell their grandchildren of the lives of saints, often situating their tales in the very places in which they live.

...whose nobility transforms the desert.

San Lorenzo de l'Escorial, Spain.

A Spanish monarch's Versailles, San Lorenzo de l'Escorial commemorates the resounding victory of the Spanish army at Saint-Quentin on August 10, 1557—the day of St. Lawrence, the martyr who was roasted alive. In his memory Philip II had the palace built in the shape of a roasting grill. The handle of the grill is formed by the royal apartments (at the back of the building) and the legs by the 180-foot-high towers at the four corners. The entire grandiose edifice, with its 16 courtyards, its 2,700 windows and 86 staircases, is rendered even more impressive and austere by the material of which it is constructed: a bluish-gray granite from the Guadarrama, which lends an air of coldness to the palace. Yet the interior of the Escorial contains many riches, such as the marble-adorned Great Chapel, which houses the gilded bronze statue of Philip II, and the Pantheon, completely lined with jasper and porphyry set off by a profusion of gilded bronze ornaments. More than anywhere else, in the Escorial one senses the spirit of mysticism and of cruelty, and above all that fascination with death, that lie at the core of all that is Spanish.

Andalusia, Spain.

The Castle of Calatayud, Spain. ▶

The poverty

of the soil enhances

the spiritual glory.

On the barren and merciless Andalusian plain flocks of sheep, the only wealth of this corner of Spain, roam seeking out the smallest tuft of grass. Lying to the east of the Sierra Nevada, the plain, covering the northern pastures of the province of Granada and more than two-thirds of the province of Almeria, is one of the most poverty-stricken regions in southern Europe. It is the home of a sparse population whose customs and dialect were deeply influenced by the Arab occupation. Wild and windswept, Andalusia is also a land of songs and dances, whose strongly eastern character influences the popular music of a great part of the Iberian peninsula.

Gaunt symbols of past Spanish greatness and present Spanish destitution, the fortresses of the Middle Ages remain as witnesses to the struggle that for seven centuries set Christian against infidel. The Castle of Calatayud overlooks the arid slopes of a hill at the foot of which nestles the Aragonese city of the same name, the Bilbilis of ancient times, which was once renowned for its weapons and its flour mills. The castle was built in the eighth century by the Moorish king Ayub, who gave it his name—Kalat-Ayub, "Ayub's castle." After the Reconquest, the kings of Aragon and Castile fought over it. Then, at the end of the fifteenth century, when nearly all the feudal castles of Spain were allowed to fall into a slow decline in favor of the capital and the port cities into which Aztec and Inca gold were flowing, Calatayud was chosen as a meeting place for the Cortes (parliaments) of Aragon and Castile, now reconciled and unified. In fact the city owes its survival to these assemblies.

Dancing the "sardana," Spain.

...that maintains reverence

for the ancient heritage...

The age-old "sardana," exalted by Homer himself, has endured through more than 2,000 years of Mediterranean history as pure as it was at birth. The traditional, intricate choreography that characterizes this slow ballet actually conveys a hidden poetic message. Greek in origin, and now the national dance of Catalonia, it begins with an "introïto" imitating a cockcrow, played on the "fluviol" (a kind of pipe). This is followed by eight short quiet steps that evoke the calm of the evening. Then sixteen long and lively steps announce the joyful end of the movement which symbolizes the sun's triumph. The charmed circle of young men and women, their hands entwined, moves now to the left, now to the right, interrupted from time to time by a sudden trill of birdsong on the "fluviol." There is no passion in the "sardana." Noble, sensual, it binds the dancers to the ground—they must always keep one foot on the earth.

Outpost of embattled Christianity, the Spanish castle of Peñafiel stands in the province of Valladolid like a milestone marking the road of the Reconquest. It rises on a barren hill at the gates of the double walled city (the walls total forty miles in all). Founded by Sancho Garcia in the eleventh century, rebuilt by Juan Manuel in 1307, completely lacking in luxuries or even rudimentary comforts (in contrast to the magnificent palaces built by the Moors in Granada or Córdoba), Peñafiel is the archetype of those strongholds erected by a Spain fighting for its deliverance, in which monks and monarchs lived austerely and without distinction as to rank or class, united by the common goal beyond any concern for protocol.

The Castle of Peñafiel, Spain. ▶

The royal cloister of the monastery of Batalha, Portugal.

Procession at Esposende, Portugal. ▶

...and drapes

the children

in the folds of

legend.

An important and well-endowed center of Manueline art, the cloister of Batalha, where in the sixteenth century all Portuguese architects were trained, is one of the richest and most beautiful in the peninsula. It owes to Boytac, "Master of the Royal Works" in the reign of Dom Manuel (1495-1521), its elegant arcades whose apertures were inspired by the wooden latticework used in front of windows in Arab lands. The royal cloister is part of the Monastery of Santa Maria da Vitoria, built in honor of the Virgin by King João I, in gratitude for her support at the battle of Aljubarrota (1385) against the Castilians. The construction of the different buildings extended over two centuries (from 1388 to 1525 approximately). Several architectural styles are mingled in Batalha, from English-inspired Gothic under João I, to the Renaissance style under João de Castilho. It thus presents a splendid guide to Portuguese architecture.

Wide-eyed and innocent, these little angels, looking as though they had just stepped down from a bas-relief by Della Robbia, are participating in the procession held each August 15 at Esposende, to the north of Oporto. Unlike their Spanish neighbors, the Portuguese give their religious festivals a happy look, and each "romaria" is the occasion for dancing, singing, and fireworks. Yet piety is still present and some pilgrims fulfill their vows by climbing the steps of the long stairways leading to the shrine on their knees, or even simulate their own death, enclosed in coffins borne in rather macabre procession by their relatives.

Like

a symphony

in geometry,

the land...

◀ Aerial view of the countryside in Eure-et-Loir, France.   Field of flax near Dieppe, France.

Tractor arabesques on now-bare fields mark the completion of the harvest. The finest flax in the world, destined for the world's most durable cloth, dries in the fields at Fontaine-le-Dun, in the Caux district in France. Each "cosaque," or stack of sheaves, is covered with straw arranged so as to shelter it from the rain, yet allow the air and sun to penetrate.

A patchwork quilt of land formed in the course of centuries by generations of farmers, the Parisian basin as seen from the air reveals successive partitioning and disputes over inheritances better than would any search through a judicial record. The terrain is ideal for large-scale agriculture but in spite of this boon each individual family maintains its own small plots of land, farming them according to its own needs or desires as in ancient times: the cornfields are light in color, the beet fields dark, the alfalfa gray, while the houses with their surrounding kitchen gardens huddle at the crossroads where there is usually a well or other water supply. "The geography of France is easily understandable to the air traveler," wrote Georges Duhamel. "The characteristic division of the land into small portions brings home to the observer the innate individualism of the people."

Chartres Cathedral and surrounding countryside, France.

Salisbury Cathedral, England. ▶

...worked and beautified by man's pious tenacity...

Five times, after five fires, the Cathedral of Notre Dame at Chartres has been rebuilt again above its own ruins. Five times the people of the surrounding countryside saw its wooden timbers blaze and fall in ashes. Five times they came with their tools, their money, their skill and their love to restore to Chartres the harmony of its proportions, the unity of its style and the boldness of its statuary. And still today Parisian students, maintaining the ancient tradition of the pilgrimages, come to Chartres in huge crowds each June to pay homage to the Virgin.

England's highest steeple soars above Salisbury and the waters of the Avon. Because of the lack of water and the too strong winds at the original site on the plain at Sarum, the seat of the bishopric was moved some miles away to Salisbury. Thus the cathedral was built on a new site and all at one time. In the nineteenth century a group of architects, displeased with the cathedral's austerity, undertook to render it "Gothic," according to the fashion of the times. They could not spoil, however, its soaring spires and its high, narrow windows that allow sunlight to enter.

is transformed

by resplendent works

of art, wedding

technical prowess

to the grace

of the past.

Reflected in the waters of the Cher, the Castle of Chenonceaux was nicknamed by posterity the "castle of women." The first works there, from 1513 to 1525, were supervised by Catherine Briçonnet, while her financier husband was off with the armies in Lombardy. The king's favorite, Diane de Poitiers, had the bridge built, designed the gardens, contrived a maze and planted 9,000 feet of strawberries. Queen Catherine de Médicis gave parties there: "The fairest and most virtuous ladies of the Court being half-naked and with their hair flowing loose like brides were employed to serve as serving maids along with the queen's daughters." Henri III's inconsolable widow, Louise de Lorraine, sat weeping over her embroidery at her window overlooking the water. The wealthy Mme. Dupin invited a thin, unknown young man, Jean-Jacques Rousseau, to teach her children there. "In this beautiful spot," he wrote, "I am becoming as fat as a friar."

◀ Castle of Chenonceaux, France.

A mathematical poem, the Tancarville Bridge, Normandy, is just under 1,200 yards long: its center road measures 665 yards; the towers rise almost 400 feet above the ground, and the roadway is 41 feet wide. Its four lanes can handle 30,000 vehicles daily. Begun in 1956, this longest suspension bridge in continental Europe was opened in July, 1959. It accelerated the economic development of the lower Seine Valley, and increased the flow of traffic between Le Havre and the western regions of France.

Tancarville Bridge, France.   ▶

The lonely silence

of a beautiful landscape...

On the banks of the sluggish Loire, strewn with sandbanks that peep above the surface of the water, the Benedictine Abbey of St. Benoît was renowned throughout Europe as a cultural center from Charlemagne's day down through the Middle Ages. The relics of St. Benedict were brought there in 672 after the destruction of the monastery on Monte Cassino by the Lombards. The abbey, which welcomed Joan of Arc who had come there on a pilgrimage, boasted some well-known commendatory abbots, including Francis I's chancellor, Cardinal Duprat, Sully and Richelieu. Beneath its splendid portal, whose capitals decorated with Biblical subjects juxtapose pillars of Corinthian inspiration, pilgrims rested and slept at the end of their long journeys. Sacked, except for the church, at the time of the French Revolution, St. Benoît's is again in use as an abbey which the Benedictine monks still devote themselves to restoring.

Abbey of St. Benoît-sur-Loire, France.

◀ Josselin Castle, France.

Calvary of Tronoën, France

...embellished by pathetic or grandiose relics...

A bastion of feudal Brittany, Josselin, which bears the name of the son of Guéthe-noc, Count of Porhoët, its original builder, has the rough-and-ready charm of all structures originally built by warriors. On the courtyard side, the granite is as finely sculptured as the softer stone from the Val de Loire. But on the side facing the valley of the Oust, from which all enemies, whether Breton or French, appeared during the war of succession in Brittany, its great blocks of stone made it an impregnable fortress. In 1629, Cardinal Richelieu had five of its nine towers and the keep demolished. To the owner he said: "Sir, I have just sent your skittles flying."

A catechism in granite, the Breton calvaries, all deeply moving in their sorrowful realism, recall episodes in the life of Christ. At Tronoën, above the Bay of Audierne, ever since the fifteenth century, the people of the district have prayed before these robust sculptures in which stone saints and knights throng around the figure of the Savior in a truly medieval rendition of life. On the third Sunday in September, crowds of Bretons dressed in regional costumes and accompanied by their children, their aged, their sick, and once upon a time by their animals (but now by a host of tourists), pay the three crosses the homage of a partly religious, partly popular "pardon."

159

Stonehenge, England.

Carnac, France. ▶

...encourages myth and superstition...

Derelicts on the wide chalky plain of Stonehenge, these great slabs of stone, once hidden under tumuli, were probably dedicated to the worship of the sun. These megaliths—the oldest known architecture of the peoples of pagan Europe—date from the time of the Bronze Age and bear witness to a civilization which had already made considerable progress. Constable (during a storm) and Turner (at sunset) both painted the fantastic arrangement of these giant monoliths topped by stone lintels similar to those of the temples at Mycenae.

Pointing to the heavens, the 2,935 megaliths at Carnac in France were erected 4,000 years ago by men equipped only with their bare hands, and are mere remnants of a far greater whole. Their considerable number attests to the density of prehistoric settlement in this area. Oriented astronomically, these monuments mark with almost perfect accuracy the position of the setting or rising sun at the solstice as well as the points of the compass. The weird character of these rows of stones has kindled man's imagination through the centuries and given birth to many superstitions and legends.

160

...and the friendly union of hearts close to nature.

A horse, a dog and—Dingle is the nostalgic dream of the thirty million Irish scattered over the world. Dingle, the farthest west one can go in Ireland, is a little Irish town, once the center of a thriving trade with Spain. Here, the country folk discuss the only event in the year that really interests them: the annual Horse Show of the Royal Society of Dublin. Not that they will go to it, however. If one lives in Dingle, where else would one want to go, where is the grass greener, the gentle hills more beautiful, or the sea air fresher? If one must leave Dingle, one might just as well leave Ireland.

Country around Dingle, Republic of Ireland.

Durham Cathedral, England.

Piously clustered

in a gentle way of life...

From the protection of their towers, the monks of Durham Cathedral, in 1346, watched the vicissitudes of the Battle of Neville's Cross, on which their fate depended. Their bishop, the Archbishop of York, was fighting alongside the English barons against the King of Scotland. To the great relief of the religious community, the Scots were defeated, and the monks could get on with the building of the church, begun in 1093 during the reign of William II, or "Rufus." Durham was still under construction at the time of the Renaissance, but its stocky outline remains representative of the Norman style brought across the English Channel by the invaders. Immediately recognizable is the method of alternating pillars, used by the builder of the nave in the Benedictine abbey at Jumièges in France.

Lying some eighty miles from London, Bibury is the cradle of a school of painting. Lying in a quiet Gloucestershire valley and deserted by its traditional population, Bibury is a retreat for painters and sculptors. On Sundays, anglers and photographers line the River Coln, teeming with trout, which flows past the sixteenth-century almshouses.

Almshouses at Bibury, England. ▶

...surprised

at work

by the Angelus...

Above the roofs of Cochem, villagers climb the hillsides to gather bunches of firm, barely ripe grapes with which to make their magnificent dry wines: Zeltinger Schlossberg and Bernkasteler Doktor. Below them lazes the Moselle, lazier still since recent canalization schemes which have depleted its waters. Cochem, nestling around its old castle which was rebuilt between 1869 and 1877, is one of the many picturesque little towns scattered along the Moselle, overlooked by the walls of their legendary fortresses and the belfries of their churches.

Moselle Valley, Germany.　　　▶

...that tolls

across the gently

rolling land...

Hemmed by trees and bushes, the hills of Gernsbach give the landscape a pastoral look. Anyone walking through the German countryside can easily get away from the beaten track and wander over these gentle slopes and meadows. Behind them flows the Rhine and in front is the Black Forest, whose treetops rise through the evening mists. It is a scene of gentle melancholy. No wonder it inspired Wagner, overcome with emotion, to say: "O my splendid fatherland. . . O enchanting German dream, dream of woods, dream of evening. . . of the village bell tolling the curfew!"

Around Gernsbach, Germany. ▶

Girls on the island of Marken, Holland.

...each village, bursting with health and color...

Fair-haired dolls of Marken Island on the Zuider Zee, these little Dutch girls are wearing the same brightly colored skirts and the same embroidered bodices that their mothers and grandmothers wore for countless generations. This unusual survival of ancient fashions in no way deprives the people of the advantages of modern living, from refrigerators to social security, and all the comforts so appreciated in the Netherlands.

Like sails on a sea of tulips the windmills of Holland, those indispensable accessories of folklore, have for centuries pumped into canals water from the marshes and lands reclaimed from the sea, ground corn, sawn wood and powdered tobacco. Once the economic driving force of an entire nation—to appraise a Dutchman's wealth, you said he was twenty-windmills rich—the windmill, now dethroned by modern machinery, remains one of Holland's most picturesque attractions.

◀ Tulip field near Haarlem, Holland.

...pursues,

and modernizes,

the ancient tasks.

Land without borders, perpetually tossed between East and West on the waves of history, Poland's agriculture is concentrated on its great central plain, a prolongation of Europe's northern plain. Wheat and beets grow in abundance in its brown earth. Possessed of an almost miraculous will to live, Poland has more than once been within an inch of being lost forever. After the great partitions, the treaty of 1795 even stipulated the complete eradication of everything that would "call to mind the existence of the kingdom of Poland." And even after the destruction wrought during the heroic Warsaw uprising of 1944 Poland managed to live again.

Harvest at Cukowowa, Poland. ▶

Swedish girl.

Lake Ottsjön, Jamtland, Sweden. ▶

Mirror of the lake

the dreaming

Nordic soul...

Melancholic and brooding, the modern Swedes are widely held to suffer from an inner disquiet. From author August Strindberg to film maker Ingmar Bergman, artists have tried to define the nostalgic despair that periodically seizes them. Yet Swedish society is probably the best organized, the most progressive, the least inhibited in the world.

The midnight sun and the aurora borealis intermingle in the sky over Jamtland, at the northern tip of Europe. Here, at latitude sixty degrees north, gorgeous meteorological phenomena are witnessed only by the vast, desolate, mirror-like lakes left behind by the Ice Age. These landscapes are on the scale of Jules Verne's wildest imaginings: "The liquid plain, colored by the vaguest shades from over the seas, was strangely transparent and endowed with an incredible dispersive power as if it had been made from carbide of sulphur. . . . It looked as though the polar basin was lit up from underneath like an immense aquarium. Some electric phenomenon, produced in the depths of the oceans, probably illuminated its most remote layers."

Swedish belfry.

...nourished on the distorted

legends of the forest...

Standing on stilt-like wooden legs, the belfries of Swedish churches bear the bells which mark the cycles of village life. Their height, which may reach up to 130 feet, is determined by the distance at which people in nearby hamlets live. Built in Ostergotland by carpenters, some of whom signed their works—Pal Personn was one—these belfries, the earliest of which date from the eighteenth century, are the most elaborate productions of a civilization which expressed itself almost exclusively in wood.

Pagodas of the west, the "stavkirker" of Scandinavia bear witness to an art that was original but short-lived. From the eleventh to the thirteenth centuries, the Vikings built a thousand churches in much the same way as they built their longships: with their axes and augers and the trees of the forest. Today no more than thirty have escaped the ravage of fire. Inside these rough, austere buildings, whose multiple roofs soar heavenward but whose floors rarely cover a surface greater than 24 square yards, all the decorations cluster around the portal which is adorned with stylized animal motifs. Pagan reminiscences rub shoulders with Christian symbols; dragons and crosses mingle in the wood just as they did in those minds the new faith had not yet conquered.

◀ Hoprekstad Church, Vik, Norway.

Castle of Olavanlinna, Savonlinna, Finland.

Black Forest, Germany. ▶

...whose stern profile floats upon the waters...

Tightly bound bundles of logs float on the Finnish waters past the forbidding Olav Castle. Built between 1475 and 1477 by Erik Aksels, it was, in the course of the following four centuries, besieged, enlarged, captured, recaptured, and bargained over by Russians, Finns, Danes and the Swedes, before finally becoming what its appearance destined it to be from the beginning—a prison. Restored after a fire, it is today a museum filled with souvenirs of war, where young Finns come to learn of their nation's troubled past, and of how difficult it is to be an independent people.

Like the bars of a giant prison, the firs of the Black Forest cast a gloomy twilight on the forest floor even in broad daylight. Their dense mass has kept man penned in the valleys, and only gangs of woodcutters can be heard working high up here on the hillsides. The solitude and mysteriousness of the German forests largely explain the Germans' religious inclinations, which were evident as early as the age of Tacitus: "They regard the woods and groves as sacred, and give the name of divinities to that mysterious character of which their veneration alone makes them aware."

Lapp children.

...observes in fascination

the crowns of the polar kings.

Children of a race threatened with extinction, these young Lapps will have to choose between the technical civilization on their doorstep and the ancestral customs of their traditional pastoral life. For centuries the Scandinavians have pushed them ever northward, to lands that allow them a bare subsistence but which at the same time guarantee the preservation of the individual character of their traditions and language. Now the time to choose between two ways of life is at hand, and in many cases the choice has already been made, since women and children now prefer to go by airplane rather than follow the head of the family on foot during the long migration of the reindeer.

Like a moving forest invading the polar corral, reindeer, most of which normally roam free, are herded together for the Vendemia at Juari in Finnish Lapland. This is the time for each owner to check his stock, select animals for slaughter and choose those which will be gelded and used as draft animals. The reindeer is the base on which the Lapp economic system is built, playing much the same role as the camel in the desert. Without the reindeer, man would probably have been unable to exist in these extreme northern latitudes.

◀ Reindeer in Finland.

THE CITIES

BY

PIERRE DE BOISDEFFRE

Today, as yesterday, the city stands for civilization. To the unchanging rhythm of the seasons, almost on the fringe of history, the farmer leads an existence that has remained basically the same for thousands of years. But the city, hectic and ever changing, raises the standard of the future. It has another privilege: in the mirror of its ancient stones it offers us the images of a vanished past. Such is the treasure of the European city—when age and wars have spared it; it is a microcosm in which each civilization has left its venerable relics . . . museum-cities, to which the world turns in quest of beauty and order, but also living cities that have refused to yield before a violent and changeful history.

When we think of Europe, we think first of those cities whose charms are all but miraculous. Cities in which a prince or a ruling dynasty often established an order that democratic passions might have disrupted. Florence is the work of the Medicis as Mantua is of the Gonzagas or Verona of the Scaligers. Versailles obeys the still more imperious order of Louis XIV, Leningrad that of Peter the Great. In a single square one can read a city's entire destiny. So it is with the Piazza della Signoria—perhaps the finest museum in the world, because the masterpieces it exhibits are not, as elsewhere, shut away from the sky and the trees that were present at their birth. One must (as André Suarès lyrically expressed it in his *Journey of the Condottiere*) choose a night in May, when the hours are blue and embroidered with old silver, to discover Florence: "I arrived in the city of the flower in the middle of the night . . . . Here and there I recognized stones and the outlines of buildings, those lasting faces. And in giving each one its name, I found them more beautiful than anything I had been told about them. Suddenly, in the Piazza della Signoria, when I saw the tower of the Palazzo Vecchio right there in front of me, I took wing, I was a gull."

It is difficult to love both the geniuses who stir your heart and their exact opposites. Vasari found Lippi's pictures barbarous; Michelangelo, in his flinty old age, cherished a relentless hatred for the triumphant Raphael, and Tintoretto had forgotten Giotto. But Florence unites these brilliant opposites: Donatello and Michelangelo live there in the same dwellings, Botticelli's Venus holds out her hand to the Venus of Titian, and Machiavelli rests, in the Church of the Santa Croce, alongside Dante. The figures in the shadows reveal themselves the equals of those gilded by the light of day, and Michelangelo fixed in marble, for the unfinished tomb of Lorenzo de' Medici, their immovable balance.

One detail: the heart of Florence—the Pitti Palace excepted—would just about fit into the area of the Louvre. How fortunate a city is when a few steps circumscribe wonders that elsewhere one would be forced to go a thousand leagues to seek . . . !

Life is long in Florence. I knew Papini there when he was almost blind, and the fresh and lucid old age of Berenson. In the French Institute, a little man, alert and goateed, told me he had followed Taine, in all the splendor of his grave and sad glory; and guided André Suarès, that young man with the face of a Christ under his astonishing arch of hair . . . . In 1945, the Arno was one of the antitank ditches of Kesselring's Gothic Line. From San Miniato, British officers watched through their field glasses as German troops ran along the cornice of the cathedral. All the bridges were blown up save one: the Ponte Vecchio, which Hitler ordered spared. When I reached Florence, virtually everything was in ruins, from the Porta Romana to the Church of San Stefano; today everything has been rebuilt, and this beautiful new stone, with its rugged and golden texture, admired in the Pitti Palace and the Palazzo Vecchio, used again in the modern constructions, has already become part of the scenery. Such is Italy's entire history, the struggles between Florence and Siena, Genoa and Pisa: men fought at the gates, a part of the town was burned down, towers were toppled, and now, ten years later, everything has been rebuilt by these indefatigable ants.

I have not space enough to describe so many splendid memories. Yet let us cite Siena and its shell of pink gold, transformed to a purple flower by the setting sun; the three monuments of Pisa, a fragile alabaster sanctuary in a setting of lush grass (where the Church of San Stefano, hung with Turkish banners, golden prows and ships' lanterns, evokes the naval battles of days gone by); Palermo, baroque and Mozarabic; the blessed triangle of Gubbio, Arezzo and Urbino . . . . Perugia with its Money-changer's House and its cool Galleria. Everywhere here, history speaks.

The Piazza Sordello, in sordid and royal Mantua, is not only a Shakespearean setting in which one could stage *Othello, Romeo and Juliet* or *King Lear,* it is a magic mirror in which one sees, arising from the very depths of history, the daughter of the Theban soothsayer, landing after the long voyage that banished her for ever from the eyeless Oedipus; or the Gonzagas, daggers in their hands, wresting power from the Bonaccossis; or Duke Guido crowning Petrarch with the wreath of laurels; or cardinals on horseback, led by Pius II, on their way to the Council.

Then there is ravenous Milan, the true capital of Italy, which met almost the same fate as London: the Palazzo Marino, the Royal Palace and the Alessi Hall were destroyed; the Palazzo Spinola, the Teatro Manzoni and the Poldi Pezzoli Museum were burned; the Church of Santa Maria delle Grazie (with Leonardo da Vinci's *Last Supper*) was devastated. But the real Milan is hidden somewhere between the Church of San Ambrogio and the Castello Sforzesco, the cradle of the city, and its spirit can be glimpsed from one Romanesque church to another.

Elsewhere, it was not the prince's palace that was the nucleus around which everything else developed; it was the sanctuary to which pilgrims flocked, from Santiago de Compostela to Nuestra Señora del Pilar, not forgetting the churches of Assisi, grouped around a sun-drenched hill.

Let us pause a moment in Spain, a land of nobility and grandeur, yet with a note of cruelty that sometimes becomes savagery. In Toledo, a striking natural setting in which a tragic history bleeds, the heart of El Greco still beats in the half rustic little house, in which the low seats, leather chairs, study tables, country-style tiling and portraits combine to create a mysterious intimacy.

Burgos Cathedral is a splendid and inexhaustible gospel of images. Córdoba is a corner of Africa and Islam on European land; Seville keeps the Patio de los Naranjos, that black-and-white checkerboard where the subjects of the Ommiads would come for their ablutions in the fountain torn from the cathedral of the Visigoths (itself built on Roman ruins), and those shaded gardens of the Giralda where one can taste a fragile peace, a contentment wrested from the convulsions of history; Granada is unique, and its cathedral is no less astonishing than the Alhambra. At Salamanca and Valladolid, splendid universities attracted, as strongly as Paris or Bologna, the turbulent swarm of students. Between venerable walls, of bricks baked and baked again by the sun, in patios sown with bright flowers and spurting fountains, in the shade of plateresque façades, it has always been good to live and dream.

Similarly Oxford and Cambridge, Heidelberg and Göttingen, Aix-en-Provence and Bologna . . . so many places where one would say that the human spirit, passing through its generations of young men, has permeated the very stones.

Between Oxford, where high medieval chapels are embedded in a modern city that grew up after the Morris works were founded at Cowley, and Cambridge, a university set amid greenery, the contrast is striking. The jagged spires and Gothic perpendicular of Oxford, the ceiling in the Divinity School and the altarpieces in the Ashmolean Museum, stand in sharp contrast to the classical pediments, the colonnades and the gleaming Backs along the Cam; it is as though the art of Oxford were medieval, reaching toward heaven, and the art of Cambridge classical, exulting in the richness of the earth.

Cambridge's artistic autonomy cannot be found at Bologna, Aix or Montpellier, real cities where the past is not isolated from time for the sole pleasure of the eye, but emerges on an active and seething life, open to the future. This is especially true of Bologna, a superb metropolis, more active than Florence, more beautiful than Milan, where the waves of passers-by and cars beat against the arcades of its red palaces and the bases of its medieval towers. Dijon could be the same, if three centuries of juridical and parliamentary life had not forced all its energies inward, so much so that it has not yet succeeded, like Grenoble or Bologna, in transforming itself and assuming the rank of a regional capital.

Which, tomorrow, Aix-en-Provence will be. No less than Dijon, capital of the Dukes of Burgundy, Aix-en-Provence, the city of Sextius, fell into a middle-class slumber (once the splendors of good King René had passed) from which it seemed unlikely ever to awaken: a museum-city, clustered about the sumptuous Cours Mirabeau, with its cathedral, where Nicolas Froment's *Burning Bush* blazes, its Palais de Justice, and the many old houses that surround the Church of Saint Jean de Malte. But it is awakening today. Its colleges dot the countryside, and from all over the world travelers flock to this Latin Greece (as pure as, but warmer and more pleasant than its ancient prototype) at the foot of that Mont Sainte-Victoire whose imposing nobility Cézanne expressed. Another metamorphosis was that of Nice. Our own fathers never suspected that it had a future outside of tourism—that it would become a Mediterranean San Francisco with its own high-yield industries, research laboratories, electronic factories; IBM's splendid concrete X is already the standard-bearer. In the twentieth century, economic and demographic development should no longer be fatal to a city of art and history. Bruges itself, which had drifted toward general paralysis following the silting-up of the Zwin, is no longer the ghost town celebrated by Rodenbach, and Ghent with its three belfries is even more lively. We may miss the Vieux Port of Marseilles with its network of alleys that recalled the Casbah in Algiers, but we must admit that the city had everything to gain by coming to terms with its century. The city hall and the little castle of La Magalone, both by Puget, figure, with the Château d'If, among the rare relics of the past. The port is constantly growing, stretching its tentacles toward the Étang de Berre, giving an impression of intense life that can be as intoxicating as alcohol.

This seething human magma is immersed in a landscape of extraordinary beauty. The Étang de Berre at the little town of Martigues, extolled by Maurras, the two ranges of the Étoile and Saint-Cyr, the masses of Marsillaveyre and Puget, invaded by deep fjords, form a natural fortification around the city, while to the east the mass of Sainte-Baume raises its tawny fleece, as it did when the Greeks landed here.

Marseilles is an Oriental suburb, but Genoa is a royal city that once reigned over almost the entire Mediterranean. With its impressive new neighborhoods, its New York-style tunnels, its shops, its banks and its endless docks and factories that extend east and west, it seems a capital beside a provincial Marseilles, lingering around a touching and obsolete basilica. And yet Marseilles today is more engaging than Genoa; the filth of Genoa's wharves is irritating while that of Marseilles is somehow appealing; Genoa's Via Balbi and Via Garibaldi, so justly praised, only fill one with coldness and resentment. The mountain is so close to the sea that a feeling of oppression results; the city lacks that gentle hinterland which gives Rome and Florence their charm. And then, the approaches to Genoa are sixteen miles of factories, dockyards and railway stations calculated to discourage the best-disposed visitor, who looks in vain for Andrea Doria's double line of fortifications. Galeazzo Alessi, who set his mark upon the finest buildings, brought to them the faults of his master, Michelangelo, without the latter's greatness. So these monuments that filled Rubens and Van Dyck with enthusiasm—the Palazzo Rossi and the Palazzo Bianco, destroyed twenty years ago and since reconstructed with splendid attention to detail—leave us cold. The mixture of styles, so frequent in Italy, if it spares the Greek cross of the Church of Santa Maria, transforms the black Cathedral of San Lorenzo, while San Ambrogio disappears under marbles, mosaics and overwhelming gilt.

The painter-kings of Genoa are those of a rich class, and they forgot the austerity of their Tuscan or Lombard masters of the great period. When one leaves Titian, Rubens and Van Dyck, one falls into the proud and empty phraseology of Guercino, into the sentimentality of Guido Reni or Dolce. The famous Campo Santo, with its neoclassical or neo-Gothic monuments, pushes this taste for décor and draperies to the absurd. In contrast, the new city, in which Mussolini gave useful knife strokes to the architecture of the nineteenth century, is grandiose. It could serve as an example to Marseilles or Lyons. Has not everything been said and written about Lyons, which some call the least habitable of French cities, and the most austere? Yet what a splendid natural setting! Two rivers between two hills, two thousand years of history, houses five centuries old, a fine park . . . perhaps Lyons will one day shake off its present reputation?

Let us go northward. Strasbourg is no better placed than Lyons. But what splendor! Two occupations and the havoc of the last war could not destroy this child of Germanic vitality and Latin genius. There remain the old hospital with its venerable woodwork, the hostelries where Voltaire and Turenne stayed, the small wooden houses of "Little France" and the sumptuous eighteenth-century red stone mansions of the Broglie or Rohan families.

And of course there is the cathedral . . . . Yet Strasbourg is not a museum-city, but a thriving metropolis, a little European capital.

Zurich is colder, richer, less likable: the height of middle-class opulence. Hamburg was severely damaged during the war; 80 per cent of it was destroyed. Yet it has retained its magnetism and found its place in the sun again. Its port is an inspiring sight. As is Bremen, which has rebuilt its wonderful square and now appears older than Munich.

I must confess to a weakness for Lübeck, for its round enameled brick towers, for its Petrikirche, still surrounded by scaffolding, for its Rathaus, a little too new perhaps, above all for its Marienkirche, which has refound its white pillars where the bricks draw narrow arteries between the walls and the whitewashed ceilings, which are enhanced by exquisite green and pink designs, like Oriental astragals. For its Cathedral of Henry the Lion, with the massive low arches of a Romanesque nave which a Christ Triumphant, in audacious polychrome, separates from the choir; for its ramparts and for its museum. The Hanseatic cities were capitals; and something of their past glory still remains. Even a capital that has fallen from its glory still retains the look of a royal city. And this is especially true of Venice, which has lost none of its incomparable beauty. Every time I go back to Venice, it is with a new emotion, and an ever-fresh surprise to note that it is still there, that nothing, or practically nothing, has moved, even though I know how fragile is the foundation on which its splendor is built; and there is no lack of plans, alas, from the Lido *autostrada* to the parking lot two steps away from the Rialto, nor of the American capital that will finance them, for the greater profit of big business and the most certain death of this city of art . . . . Nothing on earth, I think, compares with this at once mystical and sensual marriage of old marbles and turbid water, green domes and white façades, to that alternation, on the most beautiful canal in the world, of classical pediments and frail arches. Who has not dreamed of dining by candlelight in one of these palaces with its finely sculptured gilt beams, beneath ceilings by Veronese or Tiepolo? And I even know souls sensitive to grandeur who dream of drawing their last breath on the second floor of the Palazzo Vendramia, where Wagner died in the arms of Cosima Liszt.

Venice forces one to amazed contemplation of a world from which one never escapes. From all over the world men still go there and are enthralled by its inexplicable charm; a few even leave their homes and settle there. This is also true of Rome and Paris, but for slightly different reasons. Despite appearances, they are both provincial cities, and have remained such despite the waves of steel, glass and concrete that beat against the old part of the cities, and despite the assault of cars which Venice is still spared. These cities each protect very different provinces, which do not intercommunicate easily.

In Rome two capitals coexist. For the Vatican is a world in itself; it cannot be reduced to a colonnade, a basilica and a few museums around an enclosed garden: along the Via del Pellegrino are all the services, in miniature, of an established state, with its own army, postal service, radio and even its own railway station. But setting Vatican Rome to one side, there exists no apparent connection between the suburbs bristling with fourteen-story tenements whose distressing image was spread over all the screens of the world by the neorealist cinema, and those baroque palaces where poor and rich still rub shoulders, as if the industrial age and middle-class civilization had not separated the classes. The Parioli district— Rome's fashionable suburb—is farther from the densely populated Trastevere than the residential districts of Brussels or Zurich. On another plane, the "black aristocracy" of American Negro exiles rarely has anything to do with society life; it is distinct and lives apart, far from the gossip and cocktail parties of the Via Veneto.

It is not apparent that Rome had much to gain by becoming the capital of Italy. This title was more appropriate to Milan (the true capital in the economic and intellectual meaning of the word), Bologna or even Florence (which was moreover the capital of the young kingdom of Italy for a few years, before Cavour had resolved the Roman Question). Rome lost much of its poetry by increasing its area twofold and its population fourfold. Specifically, it lost that incomparable charm that was its very own when it was a provincial city sown about with closed carriages —they were still to be seen at the Conclave that elected Benedict XV—a magic garden, bordered by seven hills, where pink ruins and ocher palaces rose at random in an exuberant landscape. Mussolini managed to ventilate the Forum by laying out an "imperial" perspective there; he also mutilated the dreamlike quality that is evidenced perfectly in the smallest etching by Piranesi. In the same way, vehicles with two, three or four wheels deafen the famous walks, dishonoring the Pincio and the gardens of the Villa Borghese. Then there are the monuments. The most remarkable might well be the Capitol; the most spectacular, the Colosseum; the most perfect, the Pantheon.

Saint Peter's stands by itself, unclassifiable; the greatest opera house in the world, perfect in its proportions, with the finest cathedral in existence, whose immutable proportions have, whichever way one looks at them, a more than human splendor. What strikes the eye is not the cross, but the golden sphere that surmounts the dome and marks the temporal triumph of the pontiff. But the Tomb of Saint Peter would be even more impressive if it were open to the four winds, as Bramante and Michelangelo wanted.

As for the squares, they are known to be the most beautiful in the world. How can one choose between the perfect colonnade of Saint Peter's and the fountains of the Piazza Navona, between the small Piazza Minerva and the Farnese Market?

There are three Romes—ancient Rome, baroque and pontifical Rome, and modern Rome—but there are twenty Parises. Although the city has celebrated (albeit meagerly and in a hardly worthy manner) the two-thousandth anniversary of its foundation, there remains nothing of that "dear Lutetia" whose charms were praised by Julian the Apostate, when he came to take up winter quarters there: "The city of the Parisians occupies an island in the middle of a river; wooden bridges join it to the two shores. The river rarely rises or falls . . . one gladly drinks its clear water with its pleasant taste. Winter there is kind; a grape of good quality ripens there . . . ." Little remains of those Middle Ages, but enough for us to imagine them: Notre Dame and the Sainte Chapelle, the Château de Vincennes and the Conciergerie, a few churches, some old walls, and even some quite fine houses, to which one will add, when it has been decided to include in the Parisian agglomeration the communes that stifle it and which no plan has been able to unify, the admirable necropolis of Saint Denis. In contrast, the Paris of the Bourbons constitutes a masterly unit, of which the immense Louvre is only one of the elements; the restoration of the Marais district, which is only just beginning, is enhancing forty superb mansions, lost in a coating of apartments, shops and workshops, encrusted there since well before the end of the *ancien régime*.

There happened to Paris the opposite of what we deplore in the other capitals: although it has known war only too often and even—three times in a century and a half—foreign occupation, fighting has virtually spared it (with the sole and sad exception of the Commune, which set ablaze the Tuileries, the Monnaie and the Cour des Comptes). That is why the Parisian habitat is today the most decrepit in Europe. Worse: the city has virtually not moved since Haussmann, and we have had to wait until very recently before anyone realized the necessity of providing Paris with town planning suitable for this century.

London's case is the exact opposite. It has known no conqueror since William I, but the Great Fire of 1666 spared no stone of medieval London—with the

exception of the Tower—and the Blitz completed the weeding out of the City. Today the metropolis, with its belt of "new towns" and its rows of skyscrapers, seems somehow closer to America than to the continent. The Guildhall itself is an entirely new building, like 10 Downing Street or the House of Commons, but all have been reconstructed with that touching devotion that keeps alive institutions and customs which would have disappeared anywhere else. Thus the City's 5,180 inhabitants continue to elect two chambers in which are represented blacksmiths and pepper merchants, public letter writers and pewterers, bowmakers and leather workers—professions that ceased to exist long ago. It is true that the reality of power is not expressed in the procession that each year accompanies the installation of the new Lord Mayor, but in the revolutionary structures of the London County Council which has expropriated some 11,000 acres of land, multiplied large housing units, and thrown up around Greater London the vast belt of "new towns."

And yet there are eloquent remnants of the past. If Piccadilly Circus is beginning to resemble Times Square, Saint Paul's has found again its cold and pompous majesty, and Westminster Abbey has retained its incomparable power to move, as if poets had humanized this necropolis, ennobling even its statues of politicians. Finally, the Thames continues to bring to London the winds and fogs of the sea, and a tour of the docks is all the more impressive since the Blitz swept away innumerable little buildings that were unworthy of the district.

Paris, London and even Rome are capitals in the full meaning of the word. As is Moscow, whose vastness hides more relics of the nineteenth century than one would imagine at first sight: modest churches with onion roofs, little gardens between single-storied wooden houses, which remind us, in spite of the concrete buildings, that Chekhov's Russia is never far. And the other capitals of the North have charm and even grandeur. Of Amsterdam—the Venice of the North and unique—what can be said that has not already been said a hundred times? A museum like Delft and Venice, an economic capital like Zurich or Milan (and to all practical purposes a political capital, since The Hague is actually little more than the seat of the Court and the diplomatic corps), and above all the liveliest of cities—as well as the most enchanting, with its antiquaries, its canals, its Indonesian restaurants and its ladies of pleasure, sitting behind their glass doors like Eastern Madonnas. And, one must admit, a little debilitating too, as Camus saw well in *The Fall*.

Copenhagen, with its old harbor and its three-masted schooners which no longer serve their original purpose, and where the changing of the guard at Amalienborg Palace seems out of some operetta, leaves the traveler with the memory of a city of former times. Stockholm is grander but no less beautiful: a fine example of modern town planning that manages to inscribe its old classical quarters, spiced with a little rococo, its Governor's Palace and its House of the Nobility, the towering spire of the Riddarholm Church and the statue of Gustav Vasa in new perspectives, and to step boldly into the twentieth century without mutilating its past. Ragnar Ostberg's town hall, with its red and black colors, is the splendid symbol of this marriage of past and present. But Prince Eugen's Waldemarsudde, with its placid waters, its lawns and its weeping willows, brings an air of Watteau to the edge of the great city.

In contrast, the marriage of the two Pragues can only be termed an abject failure. The German city, heavy and deformed, made heavier still by the buildings erected during Stalin's reign, is juxtaposed to rather than integrated with old Prague, grouped on the slopes of the Royal Palace Hill. Crossing the Charles Bridge, one enters another universe: that of Maria Theresa and the Counter Reformation—which is in almost a better state of preservation than in Vienna. The gardens of Wallenstein Palace, the proud façade of Cernin Palace, where Jan Masaryk tragically met his fate, poorly-paved streets that lead up to the castle between Tuscan palaces, walled gardens and fragments of fortifications; baroque altars of the Church of Saint Nicholas, sculptures in the Convent of Loretto, and, finally, in this network of pediments and courtyards, the dazzling vault of Saint Vitus', the masterpiece of the Frenchman Mathieu d'Arras. It is difficult both to be and to have been; one can count on one's fingers the few capitals that have achieved this feat, for it requires genius.

Vienna, sad and unrecognizable, say the habitual visitors of former days, has outlived its old splendor and can no more escape from the aura of the Hapsburgs than Venice from that of the doges. They managed —and very well, too—to rebuild West Berlin, but they did not bring it to life again, and East Berlin's oppressive ruins speak more loudly than the brilliant shop windows of the Kurfürstendamm. Cities too have a soul, and a great untouched past can efface any other presence. This feeling is tangible in Leningrad, where (in spite of the October Revolution) it is enough to walk on the banks of the Neva for one's obsession with the Communist world to cease. The pure lines of the classical palaces, Prussian blue or Velásquez gray, impose on the mind the old order, whose magic is incomparable.

The speaking presence of history! Not long ago, Denis de Rougemont proposed the rebuilding of Europe, starting from town hall squares—*mairie, Rathaus* or communal house—what does it matter!

The structure of our cities has changed: the medieval city, huddled like a herd of animals around the feudal *burg,* hardly resembles our modern cities, which throw their tentacles far into the interior of the land, from dormitory villages to satellite towns. But everywhere, in Umbria as in Zeeland, in Westphalia as in Provence, in Andalusia as in Valais, history has left its mark. Europe's cities have nothing in common, for example, with the city of America's Middle West, which unfolds *ad infinitum* along an identical "Main Street" the same square blocks of buildings; nor with that of Soviet Asia, where the same "Park of Culture and Rest," decorated with polychrome portraits, red flags and statistics, can be seen near the same House of the Party, with its pseudo-classical colonnades, at the end of a giant avenue on which pedestrians look like ants. Whatever the advantages of a "functional" city, Rotterdam or Le Havre (which both had to be built anew after being almost totally destroyed) will never make us forget the ancient splendor of Amsterdam, Strasbourg or Venice. And the rebuilding of Warsaw shows that the people's democracies are not loath to honor their past!

We shall not again, alas, see the marble table before which Pierre Corneille swore his lawyer's oath, nor the old houses of Leipzig and Warsaw, of Frankfurt and Coventry. But Rouen's Palais de Justice will have restored to it, if not its old oak timberwork, at least its austere banisters and windows.

How many places there are in old Europe where there still blows, if not the spirit that Barrès celebrated from the top of the hill of Sion, at least the living breath of the past! In Barcelona, it requires only a shop window full of many-colored dolls at the side of a bustling *rambla* with its shoeshine boys to suggest the colorful splendor of the *cante jondo.* How can one fail to remember the Civil War when one sees the high walls of the Alcázar of Toledo?

In vain has Stockholm sought to imitate America: it is difficult to forget, standing before the tombs of the Riddarholm Church, that its kings once reigned over much of Europe; as for France and Italy, we are reminded of the past at each step we take . . . . "We are the only ones," cried Malraux—but that was more than a decade ago—"who no longer believe in Europe: with timid veneration the world is still regarding . . . these aged hands groping in the shadows . . . . To become convinced of it one has only to suppose Europe was dead . . . . If, on the place that once was Florence, on the spot where Paris stood, one had reached the time 'when the murmuring and stooping reeds sway,' do you think it would take long for what these illustrious places once were to become hallowed for all time in the memory of man?"

P. de B.

Château d'If, France.

The economic

prosperity

of Europe's old ports...

Bastille of the seas, the Château d'If was for centuries a symbol of royal absolutism. The walls of the old sixteenth-century enceinte and the central keep, now flanked by three towers built under Francis I, have sheltered as many legendary heroes as forgotten prisoners, from the Man in the Iron Mask to the heroes of Alexandre Dumas—Edmond Dantès and the Abbé Faria— from political prisoners during the Revolution of 1848 to a certain Monsieur de Noizelles who, because he appeared with his hat on before Louis XIV, was sent to breathe the fresh Mediterranean air here for five years. The strongly fortified citadel was never the site of any major battle, but throughout history played a dissuasive role at the approaches to Marseilles.

Heart of old Marseilles and long a retreat for poets, the Vieux Port, with its pleasure boats and restaurants permeated with the smell of the world-famous "bouillabaisse," is no longer in our day the business quarter of this ancient Phocaean city. In 1840 its docks were judged to be of insufficient depth to accommodate the new-fangled steamships, and a new harbor, La Joliette, was excavated to the north. Marseilles, standing on the site of ancient Massilia, the oldest French city, was founded in 600 B.C. by the Phocaean navigator Protis. The Greek immigration began an era of greatness that has lasted to the present day, for the "Gateway to the East" is today France's foremost port and, population-wise, its second city.

The Vieux Port, Marseilles, France.   ▶

"Man Struck by Lightning," Zadkine, Rotterdam, Holland.

...symbolized

by the power and

modernity of the world's

fleets...

"Man Struck by Lightning," the work of the French sculptor Zadkine, preserves forever on the Blaak, in the heart of Rotterdam, the memory of May 14, 1940. On that day the entire city, with the exception of the city hall, the main post office and the statue of Erasmus, was destroyed by German bombs. In 1943 the liberating Allied Forces completed the destruction of the center of the city. Ten years later another Rotterdam was born which owes nothing to its predecessor. All concrete and glass, with its skyscrapers and multilevel traffic, it is the most modern city in Europe.

Gateway of the Rhine and the second port in the world after New York, clearing almost eighty million tons of traffic annually, Rotterdam opens to the whole of Europe. One hundred and fifty cargo vessels at a time can load and unload passengers and goods along its thirteen miles of piers. In a few hours 100,000 tons of steel, coal, fertilizer, machine tools, wine, wool and spices can be handled. Rotterdam owes its extraordinary good fortune to the construction in 1872 of a magnificent waterway, the Nieuwe Waterweg, which linked it to the North Sea, thus providing ocean-going ships with an all-weather outlet to the sea.

◀ Rotterdam, Holland.

Antwerp, Belgium.

Hamburg, Germany. ▶

...perpetuates

a glorious

commercial

tradition.

Antwerp has been dedicated to wealth almost from its birth. Lyng astride the Scheldt River, a little over fifty miles from the sea, the city over which the genius of Rubens still hovers is Belgium's principal commercial port. The width and depth of the river allow the heaviest ships to sail right up to the wharves. According to legend, Antwerp was, in Roman times, under the sway of the giant Druon Antigonus, who stopped all ships sailing up the Scheldt and cut off the right hands of any sailors who could not pay him tribute. But a young relative of Julius Caesar, Salvius Brabo, vanquished him, cut off his right hand and threw it into the river. When Salvius became Duke of Brabant—still according to legend—he added to the city's coat of arms the two severed hands which still appear there today.

Bustling with excitement, Hamburg is modern Germany's foremost port, after reigning for centuries as Europe's most important financial center. With its long tradition of independence—it participated in the thirteenth century in the founding of the Hanseatic League—it only joined the Empire in 1770, and is still today one of the "Länder" of the German Federal Republic. With its black tugs sliding over the gray waters of the Elbe, their masts and smokestacks rising skyward, Hamburg, almost totally destroyed by 1945, today symbolizes Germany's truly miraculous postwar recovery.

Aigues-Mortes, France.

On what had been only a stretch of deserted sand, Aigues-Mortes sprang up in a few years. The architecture of its walls was inspired by the rectilinear plan of Roman camps, its fortifications by the circular and polygonal towers of Constantinople. St. Louis embarked from here for Egypt in 1248, and for Tunis in 1270. Then the sea receded, leaving Aigues-Mortes a prisoner of its ramparts and the sand, dedicated to less warlike pursuits. Sentries and watchmen abandoned its fifteen towers. Henceforth only carts carrying the wine of Languedoc were to pass through its ten gates.

A mystic fortress, Rhodes maintained the Cross of Christ on the borders of the Turkish Empire for three centuries. The Knights of Rhodes, divided into seven groups of "languages"—from France, Germany, Auvergne, Provence, Aragon, Italy and England—held out against all the assaults of Islam until the day in 1522 when they saw the 300 sails of the fleet of Suleiman the Magnificent approaching across the sea. They were holding their own against 300,000 besiegers, 40,000 of whom met their deaths beneath the ramparts, when an act of treachery gave the advantage to the Turks. The grand master, Villiers de L'Isle-Adam, with his 180 surviving knights, were forced to capitulate on January 1, 1523.

Rhodes, Greece. ▶

194

Dubrovnik, Yugoslavia.

prodigious fortifications...

A hybrid of Eastern and Western influences, Dubrovnik's history has been one extended effort to shake loose from its Ottoman, Venetian or Hungarian protectors and become again, as it had been in the sixteenth century, an independent republic. Then one of the richest cities of the Mediterranean, it was devastated by an earthquake in 1667. Dubrovnik was once again an autonomous republic in the eighteenth century, until Napoleon seized it and annexed it to the Illyrian provinces snatched from the Hapsburgs after the Battle of Wagram. The Emperor gave the city back its Roman name—Ragusa—and set it up as a duchy for the Maréchal de Marmont. Of this tumultuous past there remain its fortifications, in whose shelter the city snuggles, lying white and peaceful on one of the most beautiful bays along the Dalmatian coast.

A rebel city, its powerful fortifications reflected in the waters of the Atlantic, La Rochelle, the now peaceful main town of France's Charente-Maritime "département," is renowned for the stubborn resistance that this onetime bastion of the Protestant faith put up against the armies of Louis XIII in 1628. Mentioned in records for the first time in 1023, this citadel (from which the settlers who founded Montreal were to set sail), had already been bloodied by the religious struggles that marked the Reformation.

◄ La Rochelle, France.

195

...or the most romantic natural settings...

Naples and Vesuvius, Italy.

Stretching its arms over the calm waters of the gulf, exuberant Naples lies opposite a chain of volcanoes dominated by Vesuvius. Founded by Greek settlers, it became a Roman colony at the time of the Empire. It was destroyed several times and experienced occupations by the Spanish, Austrians and French, before undergoing the ordeal of World War II. An active commercial and industrial center, it is today the artistic and intellectual capital of southern Italy.

The massive fortress of the Castel Nuovo, flanked by its crenelated towers, stands on the Piazza del Municipio. It was built by Pierre de Chaulnes in the thirteenth century for Charles I of Anjou, then modified in the fifteenth century by Sagrera for Alfonso I of Aragon, and has undergone several restorations since. One of its rooms, the "hall of the barons," which was sumptuously decorated by Sagrera, is today the seat of the Neapolitan city council. The Castel Nuovo contains both fragments of frescoes by Giotto and a secret dungeon in which lie the remains of Spanish captives.

◀ Castel Nuovo, Naples, Italy.

...of familiar,

picturesque

waterfronts...

Its uncertain light which can suddenly become brilliant has attracted painters to Honfleur ever since the Romantics made Normandy fashionable. Boudin, Corot, Bonington and Jongkind set up their easels in front of the Quai Sainte Catherine and the Lieutenance. In the evening they would gather at Mère Toutain's. There, gazing on the reflections from the old harbor, they evolved Impressionism. Baudelaire, who declared that "Honfleur has always been the dearest of my dreams," wrote his poem "Invitation au Voyage" here. But in addition to being known as an artistic center, Honfleur was also the home of explorers who helped to settle Canada.

◀ Honfleur, France.

Down two hundred thirty feet of cliffs, along the banks of the Douro, Oporto displays the narrow-fronted houses characteristic of all heavily populated areas. Opposite the little café, boatmen have tied up their "rabelos," odd flat-bottomed boats with square sails and pointed bows. Ideally suited to the shallow waters of the hot season, they bring the port wine of the valley of the upper Douro to the wharves. The cellars dug out of the cliff will receive the wine and house it long enough to confer upon it the nobility which nature's bounty had already promised. From Oporto this famous wine, the region's principal resource, is exported throughout the world.

Oporto, Portugal. ▶

Grand Canal, Venice, Italy.

Ca' d'Oro, Venice, Italy. ▶

...or the sumptuous festivals of the lagoons...

An "avenue of moving crystal," Venice's Grand Canal curves gently between two rows of palaces which constitute, in the diversity of their architectural styles, what the fifteenth-century traveler Philippe de Commines was already calling "the most beautiful street in the world, with the finest houses." The city's main artery, the Grand Canal, offers an ideal setting for aquatic processions, and ever since Venice's earliest days has witnessed all manner of sumptuous and extravagant festivities, which have inspired painters and made the city a popular rendezvous for Europe's pleasure-seekers. Regattas, water tournaments and Feasts of the Redeemer recall for today's tourists the pomp and might of the Most Serene Republic of the Doges. The traditional gondolas, once the only means of getting about (there were more than 10,000 in

the sixteenth century), have gradually yielded the greater part of Venice's daily traffic to the faster but noisier "vaporetti" and "motoscafi."

Marble becomes a living plant to decorate the façade of the Ca' d'Oro, in Venice, with giant flowers. "The House of Gold" was built on the Grand Canal in 1440 at a time when the patrician families were squandering fortunes attempting to outdo each other in ostentation. It owes its name to the precious coverings of its walls, and is the most beautiful example of the Venetian Gothic style, in which Byzantine and Moorish influences mingle to good effect. The Ca' d'Oro today houses one of the most important museums in Venice.

St. Mark's and the Doges' Palace, Venice.

...everywhere

a backdrop

of high

civilization...

Inspired eclecticism seems to have governed the grouping of the buildings on Saint Mark's Square in Venice. This eclecticism is plainly evident on the façade of the basilica, that "strange and mysterious shrine, a sort of Christian mosque," as historian Hippolyte Taine called it. Built from 829 to 832 as a tomb for the body of St. Mark, brought back from Alexandria by two merchants, then reconstructed from 1073 to 1094, it was embellished over the centuries with the many gifts that the citizens of the Most Serene Republic showered upon it: precious marbles, rich mosaics dating from all periods, magnificent Roman horses dating from the fourth century B.C. and brought from Constantinople in 1204. But despite these successive and disparate additions, the basilica stands forth as one of the finest examples of Byzantine architecture.

Framed by the baroque setting of the Palladian and Byzantine overtones of the Church of Santa Maria della Salute, the triangular sails of the fishing boats remind us that Venice is a fishing port as well as an art center. At the end of the Grand Canal, side by side with the romantic gondolas so dear to Alfred de Musset and George Sand, are moored the boats. Venetians fish in the lagoon and in the Adriatic, which they reach by channels opened up through the Lido. The fish market is held a few cable lengths away from the Church of Santa Maria della Salute. One of the wonders of Venice, built in the seventeenth century in the hope that it would assuage an outbreak of the plague, the church contains some magnificent paintings by Titian and Tintoretto. But Venice is also a transatlantic port of call, and surprisingly big liners drop anchor there practically every day.

La Giudecca Canal, Venice, Italy.   ▶

Constantine IX, Mosaics, Istanbul.

...sets off the marriage between the coasts and art.

Istanbul, Turkey.

"Constantine in Christ the God, faithful King of the Romans. . ." On the great panel of the gallery of Saint Sophia's stands Constantine IX Monomachus, dressed in the imperial robes, his head surrounded by a halo intended to remind the beholder of the holy character of the Byzantine king. In 1042 he succeeded Romanus III Argyrus and Michael IV the Paphlagonian, the deceased husbands of his wife, the Empress Zoë. Skilled builders, the Byzantines considered all monuments as vehicles for decoration. In Saint Sophia's the mosaics, long hidden by Turkish whitewash, have recovered their ornamental character and again display their superb breadth in which iridescent colors and the opulence of gold bear witness to a highly refined artistic sense.

The link between Asia and Europe, built on three promontories and seven hills, Istanbul still seems to echo to the clash between Christianity and Islam. Saint Sophia's, set on the tongue of land between the Golden Horn and the Sea of Marmara, seems to represent the whole range of Byzantine history. Once a basilica, later a mosque, and now a museum, Saint Sophia's was built in 325 by Constantine the Great, not to the glory of a saint but to the glory of divine wisdom. Justinian had it rebuilt in the sixth century. For this shrine, which was to be the finest that ever existed, he sent throughout the Empire for precious materials, in particular eight pillars of green breccia marble, which probably came from the temple of Diana at Ephesus, and eight pillars originally taken from the temple of Jupiter Heliopolitan at Baalbek. Legend holds that Justinian was given the plans of Saint Sophia's by an angel.

Out of the mossy

vestiges of the past...

The dead city of Bruges they call it;
but if it is dead, it can look back on a glorious past. It reached the peak of its prosperity toward the end of the Middle Ages.
Fated by its geographic position to be
the wool mart and storage depot for the
Hanseatic cities, it became one of the
medieval world's greatest markets. Bills
of exchange and goods flowed to this
crossroads of the trade routes, where furs
from Russia intended for rich pashas crossed the path of silks ordered in the East
by Russian nobles. Ships arrived from
every country, and the shops of Bruges
overflowed with an abundance of fruit
from Granada, spices from Arabia, and
wines from the Rhine. Waxing fat by
trade, the burghers erected sumptuous
homes in which, as patrons of the arts,
they entertained artists. Giovanni Arnolfini and his wife posed here for Van Eyck's
famous painting. Van der Goes painted
his "Adoration of the Magi" here, Memling his "Last Judgment," "The Mystical
Marriage of St. Catherine" and "The
Shrine of St. Ursula." But these happy
days were numbered: the decline of the
cloth industry in Flanders and the shifting
of the great world trade routes brought
about the decline of Bruges, a decline which
was accelerated by the silting-up of its
harbor. One day in 1561 the Blankenberge
pilot announced to the city fathers that
three Spanish ships had given up trying
to dock, and were making for Antwerp.
Thereafter Bruges lived in the shadows.
But the city experienced a rebirth with
the construction of a new harbor at the
beginning of the twentieth century.

Bruges, Belgium.   ▶

...like a mirror

between identical

banks...

Laid out like a toy city where the River Limmat flows from the lake which gave it its name, Zurich has developed prodigiously since the nineteenth century. Originally a spinning center, it imported looms from England. But when Napoleon imposed his continental blockade, the people of Zurich undertook to manufacture their own looms, and did so with such success that they put them on the market. From that time on, this hastily improvised mechanical industry became one of the most important in Europe. And although in 1848 Zurich gave way to Bern as the administrative capital of Switzerland, it was able to obtain other advantages for itself: seat of the National Bank and the most popular university city in the Confederation, it is in fact, with its 400 millionaires, the economic metropolis of Switzerland.

Zurich. Switzerland. ▶

Toledo, Spain.

The Alcázar, Segovia, Spain. ▶

...each river,

at the foot

of an inspired

hillside...

"When God made the sun He set it over Toledo, whose first king was Adam," an ancient legend runs. Like a bone-dry island on the waters of the Tagus, Toledo fills to overflowing the cup of land which the river allows it. It is a dying city containing today no more than 40,000 of the 200,000 inhabitants who lived here when Toledo was a Christian outpost in a Muslim sea in the twelfth century. Endless bloody wars raged here, until nothing was left but a vast museum set out with narrow streets, tiny squares, silent cloisters and peaceful churches, all overlooked by the Alcázar, built by Charles V and demolished in 1936 in Spain's fierce Civil War.

Riveted to a rocky spur that serves as its subfoundation, the Alcázar of Segovia towers 250 feet above the natural moat formed by the junction of the Eresma and Clamores rivers. Its elongated lines and slim towers give it a fairy-tale look. Forced from the throne of Castile by his brother Don Sancho the Strong, King Alfonso VI, sovereign lord of the famous Cid, took refuge with the Moors. He thus had an opportunity to study the plans of the Alcázar of Toledo; some time later, re-established as king, he took his inspiration from it to enlarge and modify the Alcázar of Segovia, begun in the eleventh century by Abd-er-Rahman III, which later became one of the bastions of the Reconquest. As it stands today, the Alcázar probably reflects the nineteenth-century conception of the Middle Ages, for the fortress was almost completely destroyed by fire and was restored from 1882 on by the architect Bermejo.

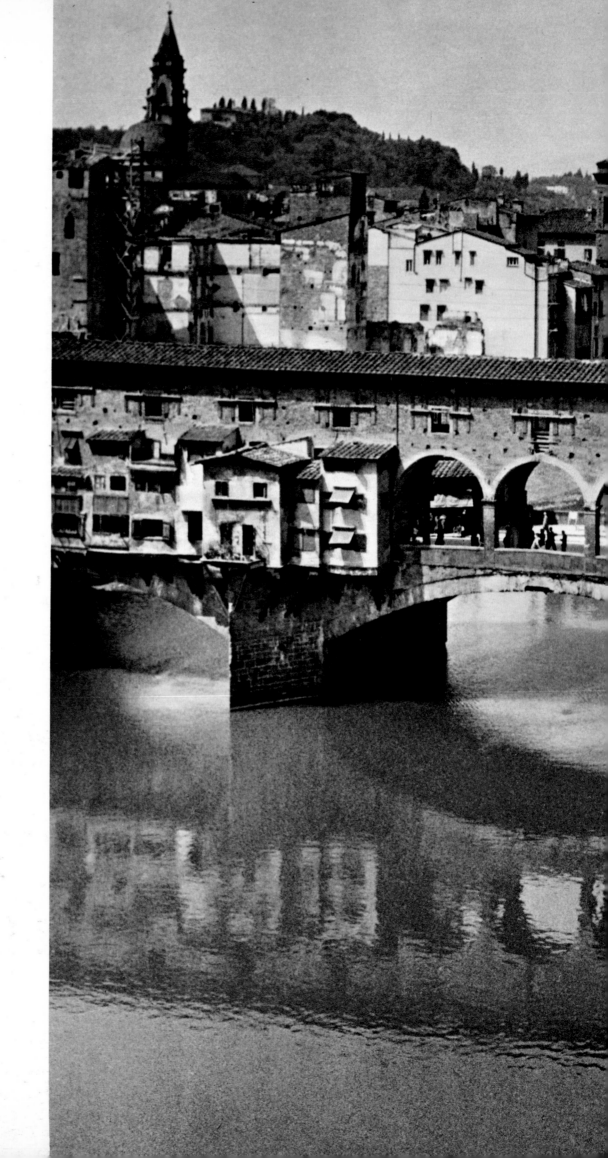

...and beneath

the stirring

overhang

of an ancient bridge...

For the pleasure of the Florentine princes, in 1345 Neri di Fioravante built a covered gallery over the Arno, connecting the Uffizi to the Pitti Palace, the residence of the Medicis. Shops, in which gold and silversmiths have been installed since the sixteenth century, run along each side of the construction, overhanging the river. The lower story was originally reserved for the common citizens, and for 500 years generations of Florentines have loitered about its central arcade which boasts a bust of Benvenuto Cellini, the "prince of silversmiths." During World War II the Germans destroyed all the bridges in the city, save this one.

The Ponte Vecchio, Florence, Italy. ▶

Stein am Rhein, Switzerland.

The Middle Ages still flourish exuberantly at Stein am Rhein, in northeastern Switzerland, not far from the hard-working town of Schaffhausen. The Sun Inn—Gasthof zur Sonne—sports a painted façade devoted to the cult of wine, its gods and worshipers. The richer a house is, the more beautiful its loggia, the more splendid its coloring and the more elaborate its sculptured decorations; some loggias even have two stories.

In the all-enveloping tranquillity of these houses slumbering along the banks of canals, the great age of Dutch painting lives again. But since the sixteenth century, Delft, Vermeer's pleasant town, has also been the center of production for a special kind of chinaware, from ordinary dinnerware to precious plaques and tiles reproducing famous paintings of the masters. It is not a native art, true, but that does not affect the popularity of its famous blue cameos showing flowers and people. It may no longer be hand-painted but "Old Delft," as it leaves the Royal Potteries today, nonetheless retains its distinctive quality.

Delft, Holland.

...reflects the growth

of Europe

through the centuries.

Avignon, France.

Three iron keys form the coat-of-arms of Avignon, but the city will reveal its charm to the visitor only if he agrees to walk through it slowly. He must cross the city walls, stroll up small streets and climb steps, cross squares shaded by plane-trees, to discover Gothic houses, classical façades, and a harvest of little churches, before coming at last to the square with its impressive sixteenth-century Gothic palace. No smoke ever rose from the palace, even though seven popes reigned here from 1305 to 1377, giving it its present splendor and making Avignon an international city. Petrarch took refuge here, and it was here that, in 1327, at the Church of the Poor Clares, he saw Laura and fell in love with her. At the end of the fourteenth century Pope Gregory XI returned to Rome. The palace fell silent, not to awaken until many years later when it roused to the sound of the trumpets at a performance of Corneille's tragedy "Le Cid." The Rhône River enfolds the city, softly caressing the crumbled arches of the Bridge of St. Bénezet before flowing on toward the Camargue and the sea.

The core of the ancient city...

Once a maritime turntable, Arles folds its tortuous streets around splendid ruins. The modern passion of bullfighting has brought new life to Hadrian's arena; in the Middle Ages this immense amphitheater, which could hold up to 26,000 spectators, was invaded by tiny dwellings before being restored to its original use. Not far from the arena is the Roman theater, built in the reign of Augustus. Only half of the original construction remains. Its tiers of seats were supported by a system of arcades, vaults and galleries similar to those of the arena. Arles also possessed the largest Romanesque nave in Provence, Saint Trophime's, whose cloister encloses some of the most sumptuous sculpture of the Middle Ages. Provence's ancient capital is now witnessing a renewal of economic vitality, thanks to the rice fields of the Camargue which are being strenuously developed.

Arles, France. ▶

...the arena is still the scene of impassioned ritual.

"**Already the bull was bellowing** at his forehead." Thus the poet Lorca, on behalf of all Spain, mourned the death of Ignacio Sanchez Mejias, one of the most famous of bullfighters. Manolete, once the idol of the "aficionados," met his death in the same way. But the arena revives after each death and each time is incarnated in its new champion. There is a strange magic to this mixture of fervor and cruelty; a poignant beauty in this contest between man and beast. Brutal, gratuitous violence, say those who are horrified by the bullring; the essence of artistic emotion, the purity of a game in which there can be no cheating, reply the others. Spanish passions erupt at each "corrida," and if Goya made its intensity spring forth, Picasso underlines its sharpness, and Hemingway its ethical values. This is the other religion of Spain, which sends man and bull to their deaths the better to extol them.

A circus of death in the valley of the Arga River, Pamplona yearly sacrifices its bulls to the insatiable appetites of the "aficionados"—and the tourists. Are the ancestors of these bulls those that were led, crowned with gay flowers, to the knife of the priest in ancient times? The origin of the bullfight is not known for certain. Some say it developed from ancient circus contests, others think it a unique product of the harsh Spanish genius. However that may be, all sides are agreed that Francisco Romero, born about 1700, was the true creator of modern bullfighting. Originally each fight was left to the inspiration of the matador. It was not until the beginning of the nineteenth century that Francisco Montes established a rigid code of behavior which decreed how the fight should be ordered. Thus the rites of the "corrida" are perpetuated, from the "paseo"—a dazzling parade of light—to the final "tercio de la muerte" in all its tragic intensity.

◀ The Bullring, Pamplona, Spain.

"Street of the Flowers," Córdoba, Spain.

"House of the Shells," Salamanca, Spain. ▶

On walls brushed by the wings of the past...

Bedecked with flowers, the walls of the old parts of Córdoba bear witness to a people's inbred taste for color, gaiety and life. Of all Córdoba's alleys, the Calle de las Flores, beneath the tower of the cathedral (once a great mosque), is the most famous. Climbing dazzling house fronts, petunias, morning glories, geraniums and verbenas overflow from these patios, where plants proliferate and appear to the passer-by as silent cool mirages behind the wrought-iron grilles.

Ostentatiously sober, civil architecture at the time of the Catholic monarchs was nonetheless bold enough to contrive the most unexpected motifs. Thus in Salamanca one sees the shells on the walls of a patrician house, the Casa de las Conchas, built for a doctor, Don Rodrigo Maldonado, at the end of the fifteenth century. The shield with the fleur de lys of the Maldonado family and the shells of the Benavente family, who were related to the founders, decorate the façade of this famous palace.

...in the stunning

arrangement

of certain jewel

boxes of art...

The Piazza del Campo lies in the center of Siena, in the Middle Ages an opulent free city which owed its prosperity to trade and to the privileges that popes and emperors vied with each other to bestow. The tower of the communal palace, built between 1297 and 1310, is more than 325 feet high. Its elegant lines harmonize with the shell-shaped square which is surrounded by houses built in a style that was then imposed on the rest of the city. Here each year are held the races of the Palio, whose origin traces back to the birth of the Sienese "contrade," or provinces. The representatives from each "contrada," dressed in fifteenth-century costume and surrounded by halberdiers and arquebusiers, form a traditional procession as they cross the city. Then the races are held on the Piazza del Campo, and the winner receives a gonfalon as his prize.

Piazza del Campo, Siena, Italy.　▶

...in a transposition of centuries at twilight...

Lying at the junction of two great rivers, Lyons has been a privileged city through the centuries. The main roads through the Alps terminate here, and both the Rhône and the Saône flow through the city, giving it its name of the "City of Bridges." In Roman times it was the capital of Gaul and later was one of the first centers of Christianity. Its great prosperity in the Middle Ages was linked to the coming of Italian bankers, who established in this city the most important fairs in Europe. Ever since that time, financiers, businessmen, men of law, and government officials have settled in the Saint Jean district, at the foot of the Fourvière hill. The modern evidence of Lyons' glorious past are these sumptuous dwellings, with Romanesque archways, Gothic windows and overhanging Renaissance turrets. In the sixteenth century the introduction of silk established the city's basic industry. In modern times the city has enjoyed a renaissance which began during the Second Empire and accelerated in the years following World War I. Today the seat of great industries and the economic and religious capital of the region—its archdiocese holds the primacy of the Gauls—Lyons, with its 800,000 inhabitants, is France's third urban center.

"Manhattan in Tuscany," its unique towers, many of them inhabited today by rich Americans, are responsible for San Gimignano's unexpected nickname. Only thirteen have survived of the seventy-three which were built in the Middle Ages to offer sanctuary during the everlasting bloody quarrels between the Ghibellines, partisans of the emperor, and the Guelphs, who wanted independence for the Italian towns under the supremacy of the pope. Each family built its own tower, whose height and elegance bore witness to the owner's prestige and rank.

The Saint Jean district, Lyons, France.

San Gimignano, Italy. ▶

...survives the venerable memory of the walled towns...

The old city, Carcassonne, France.

Finest surviving example of a medieval French walled city is Carcassonne, with its high ramparts towering above the surrounding fir trees. Flanked by twelfth-century and even Visigoth towers, topped by thirteenth-century battlements, its walls bear witness to a glorious past. The Narbonne Gate gives access to the heart of the city: moated Comtal Castle, a veritable forest of towers and turrets, vaulted Gothic halls, bartizans and machicolations. Abandoned for many years, the walled city has won renewed fame since its restoration by Viollet-le-Duc. The Aude River separates the walled city from the lower city which was built on a checkerboard pattern during the reign of St. Louis (Louis IX). The streets are laid out in straight lines that call to mind the plans of some modern American cities, but actually several examples of similar city design existed in the south of France during the Middle Ages.

Getreidegasse, Salzburg, Austria.

In the heart of the heart of Europe, said the poet, between the north and the south, between the mountains and the plains, lies Salzburg. The city has never chosen between past and present. Here it is princely baroque, there one finds a lingering trace of naïve country life. The secret of its charm, however, remains basically indefinable. The composer Mozart exhibited the best of its qualities in his works: purity, style, simplicity and grace. And always one is aware of a faint yet ever present sense of melancholy, which seems to rise from the green waters of the Salzach and radiate from the city's domes and belfries. It was at 9 Getreidegasse that Wolfgang Amadeus Mozart was born, and played his first scales. His spirit still seems to hover over the celebrated festivals which are held in the city each year.

...with the echoes of yesterday's warriors...

In the fluid light of the laughing valley of the Salzach, the citadel of Hohensalzburg was begun in the age of the struggle between the forces of church and state. The powerful archbishop-princes of Salzburg made it a veritable fortress, whose bastions watched over a double and triple ring of fortifications inside which vast stores of weapons were accumulated. In the sixteenth century they added luxurious rooms and set up residence here. The fortress had become literally a city within the city, complete with its Church of Saint George, its main square, its shops, its streets and its reservoirs. One of the lords of this archbishopric, however, Wolf Dietrich von Raitenau, became trapped by his own power, for in 1612 he was imprisoned in the fortress after being deposed for immoral conduct.

The Citadel, Salzburg, Austria.   ▶

The Piazza, Bergamo, Italy.

Urbino, Italy.

...marvels of austere or sumptuary architecture.

A splendid sepulcher in many-colored marble, the Colleoni Chapel at Bergamo is the last resting place of the famous "condottiere" Bartolomeo Colleoni. Built in 1476 by the architect Amadeo, it was later decorated by Tiepolo, who forever immortalized the memory of this general from Bergamo and his daughter Medea. Set between the austere dome of Santa Maria Maggiore and the baptistery of Giovanni da Campione, the chapel radiates a Venetian luxuriance. Amadeo skillfully harmonized these incongruous styles and made the Piazza del Duomo a masterpiece of contrasting effects.

Slumbering on its two hills, Urbino remembers the time in the fifteenth century when, under Duke Federigo of Montefeltro, it was a center of the arts and sciences, and gave birth to the great Raphael. Then, after this brilliant epoch, the tiny provincial capital closed itself up with its memories in the shadow of its ducal palace, a magnificent Renaissance building that owes its decoration to Barocci. It houses the National Gallery of the Marches, where pictures by Uccello, Piero della Francesca, Signorelli and Berruguete hang side by side.

Cathedral of Santiago de Compostela, Spain.

Glowing and made flesh

on the spandrels of churches...

A Christian shrine, Santiago de Compostela has attracted pilgrims from all over Europe since the Middle Ages. Legend has it that St. James the Greater, come to spread the gospel to Spain, disembarked in Galicia, whence he sailed back to Judaea some years later. After his martyrdom, his disciples placed his body in a boat which by a miracle beached itself on the Ulla estuary, in Galicia. Forgotten by the time of the invasions, his sepulcher was not rediscovered until the year 800. The saint then became the patron saint of Christian Spain in its struggle against Islam, and "Santiago!" (St. James) was the war cry of the Spanish troops as they stormed Moorish citadels. A cathedral, probably the work of French architects, was built in honor of the saint in the eleventh and twelfth centuries. Its architecture, like that of Saint Sernin's at Toulouse, was conceived to facilitate the veneration of its relics, the passing of processions and the coming and going of crowds of pilgrims.

The Porch of Glory of the gigantic Cathedral of Santiago de Compostela, the work of the master Mathieu, dates from 1183. If it cannot be compared to French tympana like those at Vézelay, Moissac and Conques, it is nonetheless strikingly original in its different feeling for relief and movement. Its three arches are crowded with a multitude of heavenly and earthly characters from the Old and New Testament: Jeremiah, Daniel, Isaiah, Moses (from left to right), whose names can be read on the tablets they hold in their hands, old men of the Apocalypse talking among themselves, and incense-bearing angels grouped around the Apostle James who is seated on a pillar of gray marble that represents the Tree of Jesse. In the course of centuries five holes have been worn in the marble by the hands of pilgrims, ample evidence of their fervor.

The Porch of Glory, Santiago de Compostela, Spain. ▶

...the soul of the region is expressed by every cathedral...

Limburg Cathedral, Germany.

Ulm Cathedral, Germany.

The world's highest spire, as well as the one which best displays the skill of Gothic craftsmen, rises 528 feet into the air above the splendid Cathedral of Ulm. Begun in 1377, the cathedral's construction went on until 1529. Work was abandoned then for more than three centuries, and only commenced again in 1844. It was finally completed, to the original plans, at the end of the nineteenth century.

Enhanced by the trees which surround it, Limburg Cathedral stands on the edge of a sheer cliff that overlooks the waters of the Lahn. Built between 1200 and 1275, it is one of a number of thirteenth-century cathedrals that were inspired by French models. Among its collection is a masterpiece of Byzantine art, the reliquary of the True Cross, brought back by German crusaders after the sack of Constantinople.

...the prodigal

richness

of the materials...

A remarkable display of architectural virtuosity, the white marble cathedral, baptistery and bell tower of Pisa were erected from the eleventh to the fourteenth centuries. Each of the monuments was built by a different architect, but they share the same inspiration, following a Romanesque plan, with groupings of small columns surmounted by arches. This kind of geometrical decoration is typical of what has become known as the Pisan style, the influence of which can be found at Lucca, Pistoia and even in Sicily. Pisa is one of the oldest cities in Italy. Etruscan, then Roman, it enjoyed, before its defeat by Genoa in the naval battle of Meloria, an era of great prosperity and power, to which we owe these architectural masterpieces that still astound us.

Pisa, Italy.　　　　　▶

the imagination,

the delicacy,

and the variety

of the architecture...

A priceless gift from the East to the West, the Courtyard of the Lions in the Alhambra at Granada dates from 1377. Its 184 white marble pillars, its arches decorated with stalactite-like carvings and its cedarwood friezes bear witness to the fertile imagination of the Moorish artists. Like a house of cards harassed by the wind, the frail structure has been in a process of almost continual restoration ever since the sixteenth century to prevent it from collapsing. The slightly archaic carved lions beneath the fountain lend a primitive note which preserves it from excessive opulence and refinement.

◀ The Alhambra, Granada, Spain.

"Tailladée en scie, découpée à jour comme à l'emporte-pièce, festonnée et brodée, ciselée jusque dans le moindre détail comme un chaton de bague," the steeple of Burgos Cathedral, the work of John of Cologne, left poet Théophile Gautier dazed when he saw it for the first time. Over 275 feet high, it took the craftsmen of the fifteenth century several decades to build this handsome structure which crowns a splendidly rich building, begun in 1221 by Bishop Mauricio, and not completed until more than three centuries later.

Burgos Cathedral, Spain. ▶

Graslei, Ghent, Belgium.

The mansions of rich merchants on the Graslei stand as symbols of the prosperity of Ghent, the economic metropolis of medieval Flanders. About the year 1600, the Corporation of Masons had a house built (at left) whose Gothic façade prefigures modern architecture in its simplicity. The Grain Measurers installed themselves three buildings farther on in 1698, next to the abode of the Free Boatmen who had been established since 1531 in the Gothic-style house already touched by the first splendors of the Renaissance. But the destitute had their palace as well: the house of the Cornmart, an austere Romanesque building with a façade banded by molded cordons and windows divided by a small column (center of our photograph), was used as a storehouse for the grain transported across the Lys and Scheldt rivers.

Consistent in its particularism, Strasbourg maintains a continuity with its very long history. Built of red sandstone from the Vosges, the old houses seem to stretch their mossy roofs, still pierced by the skylights of tobacco-storage attics, toward the cathedral steeple which towers upward for over 465 feet.

The crossroads of southern Germany and capital of Bavaria, Munich is one of the outstanding cultural and industrial centers of Europe. Founded about 1102 by a group of monks, it owes its importance to Henry the Lion, who had a bridge thrown across the Isar in 1158. The Gothic-style Neues Rathaus (New City Hall) was built about 1870.

Strasbourg, France.

Munich, Germany.

*...the secret troth
of the belfry
and the surrounding
rooftops...*

◀ University Library, Coimbra, Portugal.

Trinity College, Cambridge, England.

...vie in originality with the monuments of secular art.

A true palace of knowledge, the University of Coimbra is one of the great seats of learning which European humanism inspired. Its founding dates back to the thirteenth century. The library, begun in 1715 when Nuno de Silva Teles was rector and completed in 1723, consists of three halls, connected by arcades painted to imitate white marble. The walls are covered by bookshelves, the upper parts of which are crowned by rococo frontons. The library contains a million volumes and 3,000 manuscripts; among its valuable works are the first edition of the "Lusiads," an epic poem by Camoëns that tells of the Portuguese discoveries in the East Indies, a thirteenth-century parchment Bible, and Queen Eleonora's Book of Hours.

Citadel of the "Establishment," Cambridge, together with Oxford, is the cornerstone of British culture. For centuries a large proportion of the civil servants and politicians who have held the reins of power in Great Britain have been educated here. Situated on the banks of the River Cam, Cambridge, with its eighteen colleges, is an ancient university town, whose origins go back to the founding of religious schools at the beginning of the twelfth century. Trinity College (above, the Main Gate), where Byron once studied, is the most important of the colleges. It was founded in 1546 by Henry VIII and built by Neville; it rests on monolithic pillars, with a sculptured entablature, topped with a decoration in the shape of a crown.

The Erechtheum, Athens, Greece.

The Acropolis, Athens, Greece.

Through harmonious purity and grace...

etrified goddesses, the Caryatids seemingly effortlessly support the weight of the emple of Erechtheus on the Acropolis. Set on a hollow plinth some eight feet high nd fifteen feet wide, these girls, miracles of grace and nobility, proudly display their erfect bodies. They are believed to have been inspired by Ionian motifs. The uarter round of the capital that rests on their heads recalls the baskets in which the ncient priestesses carried the sacred objects. Originally six in number, only five of e statues remain—beside a bastard sister which is simply a cement cast.

High above Athens, the Parthenon stands proudly on the Acropolis, the heart of the ancient city of which it was both the sanctuary and the fortress. Despite its glorious past, Athens was nothing more than a small town when it became the capital of a Greece newly freed from the Turkish yoke in 1833. Since then, it has spread out in all directions, from Piraeus to Kiphisia, and today is a prosperous, bustling modern city. At the foot of the Acropolis, Plaka, the old part of the city, huddles between the temple dedicated to Zeus the Olympian, and the Roman Agora.

245

◀ The Colosseum, Rome, Italy.

Saint Peter's Square, Vatican City.

through the nobility of great constructions...

Papal Guard, Vatican City.

Living heart of Christendom, the Vatican City, which casts the shadow of the dome of its basilica over Rome, contains a number of architectural masterpieces within its walls. Baroque and Renaissance examples surround an 84-foot-tall Egyptian obelisk which came originally from Heliopolis and now marks the center of St. Peter's Square. In the seventeenth century Bernini constructed the quadruple row of 284 pillars and 88 pilasters, crowned with a balustrade upon which stand 140 statues of saints. These great stone sculptures lend a solemn and grandiose note to the approaches to the basilica, and at the same time mark the limits of the earthly empire of the head of the Church.

Peaceful sentries, the Vatican's Swiss Guards with their medieval halberds and their multicolored uniforms designed by Michelangelo, bear witness to the extent to which the Church has abandoned secular power in favor of the spiritual. The Lateran Treaty, signed on February 11, 1929, put an end to the "Roman Question" which was raised when Victor Emmanuel took Rome in 1870. The treaty guaranteed the independence of the Vatican City, while the Pope for his part agreed to recognize Rome as the capital of Italy.

A vast deserted theater, whose silence still summons memories of gladiatorial combats, mock sea fights and the martyrdom of early Christians, the Colosseum is one of the great architectural wonders of the world. It belongs with the fantastic make-believe constructions of Piranesi. Begun in 72 A.D. by Vespasian, it was completed in the year 82 by Domitian. Its impressive proportions, with a circumference of over 1,700 feet and a seating capacity of 50,000, caused it to be called the Colosseum even before it was finished. This mountain of stone in the heart of Rome survived all attempts at destruction. During the Italian Renaissance, it was used as a quarry for the travertine stone employed to build the palaces and churches of the Eternal City. Yet the mutilated edifice, although shaken by earthquakes and transformed into a fortress in the sixteenth century, has lost none of its magnificence.

...through the exaltation

of the religion

of Christ...

Solemnly bedecked for religious festivals, the bronze statue of Saint Peter rests on a marble seat in a recess in the central nave of the basilica dedicated to the first pope. According to tradition the statue dates from the fifth century, but it is probably the work of Arnolfo di Cambio, who lived in the thirteenth century. The caresses and kisses of millions of pilgrims from all corners of the earth have worn down the saint's right foot.

"St. Peter," attributed to Arnolfo di Cambio, Vatican City. ▶

"Majesty, what incomparable majesty!" exclaimed the Catholic writer Daniel-Rops when he beheld the time-honored order that governs liturgical ceremonies in the Basilica of Saint Peter. Bishops, patriarchs, prelates and canons, all clad in their ceremonial vestments, are seated along the sides of the nave, and the elevated throne of the supreme pontiff is bathed in light, while guards in helmets bedecked with white horsetails stand on either side. This solemn pomp which surrounds the Pope is in good part inherited from the ceremonies once held at the court of Byzantium, and has as its object the celebration of the grandeur of the Church and the exaltation of its visible head, the Vicar of Him to Whom "alone belong the power and the glory."

Ceremony in St. Peter's, Vatican City. ▶ ▶

Ceremony of the opening of Parliament, London.

...through the majestic austerity
of tradition...

The Queen of England reigns but does not rule, and the speech she reads from her throne at the opening of each session of Parliament is written by her ministers. Once passed by Parliament, projected laws are subject to a purely formal royal assent, which is still expressed in Norman French according to the ancient formula: "La Reine le veult" (The Queen wishes it). By tradition, some of which dates back to the beginning of the sixteenth century, each new session of the House of Commons must elect a Speaker, or chairman, whose authority is symbolized by a mace borne by a sergeant-at-arms in the procession that precedes the prayers at the opening of each session. In the House of Lords, the Speaker is the Lord Chancellor, whose place is a seat called the "woolsack." But this solemn setting is merely evidence of the sentimental attachment that Britain feels for its past, and in no way hinders the functioning of Britain's governmental machinery in the modern world.

A nation's watchman, the Houses of Parliament were built on the site of an ancient royal residence, and were rebuilt to the original plans after a fire caused by German bombers laid the House of Commons waste on May 10, 1941. When the House is sitting, Clock Tower, which houses Big Ben, is lit up at night, and during the day a flag flies above Victoria Tower. To the left is Westminster Abbey. Ever since Henry III, during whose reign it was begun, Britain's kings and great men have been buried here.

Houses of Parliament and Westminster Abbey, London.   ▶

...through

the glorification

of spangled forms..

"L'arche démesurée" extolled by Victor Hugo, the memorial beneath which the Unknown Soldier of World War I has lain since 1920, rises with its imposing bulk on the summit of ancient Chaillot hill in Paris. In 1806, Napoleon decided to build a triumphal arch in the capital to the glory of the imperial armies. He wanted it at the entry to the boulevards near the Place de la Bastille, but because the site was not suitable it was decided to build the monument where it stands today. Chalgrin drew up the plans and undertook their execution, then Huyot and Blouet carried on his work, which was not completed until 1836, under Louis-Philippe. Some 160 feet high and 147 feet wide, with its arch measuring 95 feet in height, it is the symbol of national honor for every Frenchman.

◄ Place de l'Étoile, Paris.

The eye of its cathedral, the rose of the south window of Notre Dame has a diameter of almost forty feet. It is the work of Pierre de Montreuil, one of the greatest French architects of the thirteenth century, and of the master glaziers who so magnificently displayed their talents on the façades of Chartres Cathedral and the Sainte Chapelle. Perfectly integrated with the light stonework that supported them, at a time when people knew nothing of artificial lighting, the rose windows illuminate the interior of the cathedral with rays of color that blend with the multi-hued decoration of the walls.

South window of Notre Dame, ▶ Paris, France.

The Grand'Place, Brussels, Belgium.   The Kaiser Wilhelm Memorial Church, Berlin, Germany. ▶

...each European

capital

is the unique

image of a faith.

A sumptuous display of Brabant baroque, the façade of the town hall stands on one side of the Grand'Place in Brussels. The highest belfry in the city, some 315 feet tall, it is a magnificent witness to the opulence of this Belgian metropolis. Built in the first half of the fifteenth century, the Hôtel de Ville is one of the finest examples of civil Gothic architecture in Belgium. In 1695, Marshal de Villeroy, seeking to free his troops who were besieged in Namur, bombarded Brussels, burning down the town hall and 4,000 houses. Rebuilt above its ruins, the edifice was forced to undergo the "improvements" of nineteenth-century architects who sought to complete its decoration by adding a great many sculptures.

The amputated stump of a belfry was all that remained in 1945 of the 370-foot-high spire of the Kaiser Wilhelm Memorial Church, built in the neo-Romanesque style between 1891 and 1895. As the ruins of their capital were gradually cleared away, Berlin's stump of a belfry took on a symbolic value in the eyes of Berliners, and the city fathers decided to leave it as it was. This solemn ruin at the beginning of the Kurfürstendamm, Berlin's main avenue, provides a striking contrast with the neighboring modern church where services are held today.

The inexhaustible springs of humanism have fertilized...

Royal bronze fountains in the Place de la Concorde spring to life at night in the glare of huge floodlights. When King Louis-Philippe asked the architect Hittorf to restore the square that had just been named Concorde, the architect chose to decorate its center with an obelisk donated by the Pasha of Egypt, Mehmet Ali, and brought straight from Luxor; he also decided on fountains modeled on those in Saint Peter's Square in Rome. He thus sought to banish the troublesome memories of the Revolution, when statues of France's kings were knocked over and replaced by the grim specter of the guillotine.

◀ Place de la Concorde, Paris, France.

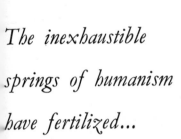

Surrounded by waterfalls and springs, Neptune emerges glorious beneath the triumphal arch that surmounts the Trevi Fountain in Rome. The work of Salvi—who probably worked from sketches by Bernini—the greatest and perhaps the most beautiful of Roman fountains was begun during the pontificate of Clement XII, then completed in 1762 under Clement XIII. It is framed by the façade of the Poli Palace. A legend has it that in former times a virgin led the Roman soldiers to the abundant springs that feed the fountain. Hence the name which was originally given to its waters: "aqua virgo."

The Fountain of Trevi, Rome, Italy. ▶

◀ The Vienna Opera House, Austria.

The Belvedere, Vienna, Austria

...secular temples of music and dance...

All the gaiety of the ancient city of the Hapsburgs, watered by Johann Strauss's "Blue Danube," lives again in Vienna's new Opera House. The world capital of music, home of Haydn, Schubert, Beethoven, Gluck, and later, Schönberg, Berg and Weber, Vienna inaugurated its Imperial Opera House in 1869 with a performance of Mozart's "Don Giovanni." During the bombardments of 1945, which razed the building, 80,000 costumes and the sets for 120 productions were destroyed. After ten years of work, the Opera House was reopened with a performance of Beethoven's "Fidelio." Each year a magnificent coming-out ball which is held in the Opera House attracts the young men and women of Viennese society.

The Castle of the Belvedere in Vienna is so huge and lavish that no one could seriously think of living there today. Built in 1714 for Eugene of Savoy, the "secret emperor" famed as the conqueror of the Turks, it is representative of the giganticism typical of Austrian architecture. Here the baroque achieved its full majestic splendor at a time when it seemed almost moribund in the rest of Europe. The architect, Von Hildebrandt, originally conceived the Belvedere as two palaces. The Lower Belvedere, the summer residence of Prince Eugene, houses two museums. The Upper Belvedere, whose vestibule with its huge atlantes can be seen above, was the site of the signing of the treaty in 1955 that put an end to the occupation of Austria.

259

The Forum, Rome, Italy.

...architectural triumphs that glorify the city...

The Eiffel Tower, Paris, France.

"Three hundred meters of uselessness! An insult to good taste!" Such were the comments of indignant Parisians at the opening of the Eiffel Tower in 1887. Since then, its existence has been partially justified by its employment for radio purposes in 1918, and for meteorology and television today. Used as a gigantic advertising billboard by André Citroën before World War II, the tower gradually became an accepted part of the Paris skyline—until it became indispensable. Artists adopted it: Jean Cocteau dedicated a play to it, René Clair let his cameras wander about among its girders, Charles Trenet dedicated his song "Paris Is the Eiffel Tower" to it. Crowds of people flock there; and tourists regard the tower as the most important of French monuments.

Relics of a splendid imperial adventure, Roman ruins throughout Europe, as well as in Africa, Syria and Asia Minor, bear witness to the unflagging genius of the builders from the banks of the Tiber. The heart of the empire, the Roman Forum was progressively covered with buildings destined for public meetings. Its decline, accompanying that of Rome, dates from the first centuries of our era. In the Middle Ages, barons built fortified towers on its hills, while livestock grazed on the Forum land, known as the Campo Vaccino, as we can see from the engravings by Piranesi and the paintings of Hubert Robert.

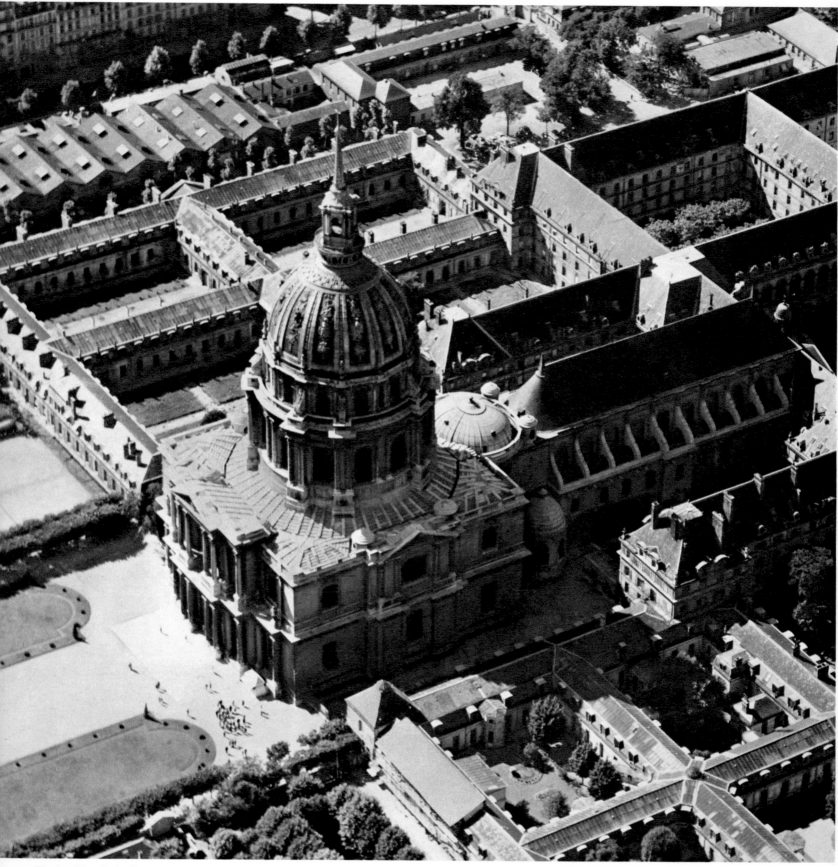

The Invalides, Paris, France.

...the splendid composition

With its patterns of sunlight and shadow alternating in rectangular courtyards and gardens, half resembling a monastery and half a barracks, the Hôtel des Invalides, built from 1671 to 1676 by Libéral Bruant, and completed by Mansart in 1677, was put to immediate use by Louvois as a hospital for soldiers wounded in the royal service. The Church of Saint Louis, called the "Soldiers' Church," whose handsomely ornamented dome rises above a building decorated with poised columns, is by contrast a sumptuous monument. It was here that on December 15, 1840, Napoleon was interred. His sarcophagus, carved from a single block of red porphyry, and placed in a circular crypt excavated in the center of the church, was completed twenty years later.

St. Paul's Cathedral, London, England.

of ancient monuments...

A massive cowl towering above the tightly packed buildings of the City of London—the Roman Londinium—the cupola of Saint Paul's Cathedral rests on eight pillars. But in its base, invisible, it is reinforced by a giant chain embedded in the masonry. Therein lies the ingenuity of the architect, a young amateur of great wisdom, who had the task of rebuilding fifty churches in the City ravaged by the Great Fire of London. To support an 800-ton dome, Christopher Wren, with the same brilliance, conceived of setting it on a cone of bricks disguised under an exterior dome. With the commonest of materials—brick, plaster, iron and stone—he managed to build a cathedral that departed from the well-worn path of English Gothic, a cathedral that is often compared to Saint Peter's in Rome.

Schönbrunn, Austria.

The ghost of l'Aiglon—the Little Eagle—Napoleon's son, who died here in 1832 at the age of twenty-one, roams the vast imperial palace of Schönbrunn where another illustrious child, Mozart, gave a concert when he was only six. The palace, formerly the residence of the court during part of the year, owes its name to the nearby spring that the Emperor Mathias discovered in 1605 while hunting: Schöner Brunnen, or "Beautiful Spring." Destroyed during the Turkish siege in 1683, the palace was rebuilt after plans by Fischer von Erlach, but it was during the time of Maria Theresa, in 1750, that it acquired its present appearance. The Empress laid out the gardens and built a summer house on the hill behind the palace. Napoleon twice stayed at Schönbrunn, where he signed the treaty of the same name in 1809. Franz Josef was born here in 1830 and died here in 1916.

...the sumptuous growth of lordly mansions...

Regional costumes, Central Moravia, Czechoslovakia.

A land where folklore comes alive, Czechoslovakia offers on each of its important holidays an occasion for country folk to don their picturesque traditional costumes. There is singing and dancing until midnight, even in the cities, where people from the same district gather together. Actually the Czechs had developed a well-defined industry while their provinces of Bohemia and Moravia still belonged to the Austro-Hungarian Empire, but the Slovaks are still closely bound to the land. The languages of the two peoples are closely related, only about a thousand words and some slight variation in pronunciation (softer and more musical in Slovak) differentiating between the two tongues.

...the subtle harmony of peoples

and the shrines of the spirit...

Romanesque, Gothic, Renaissance, baroque, all styles telescope and overlap in the jumble of buildings of the Hradschin, the Royal Palace in Prague. Each king of Bohemia, starting with Charles IV, added to it and altered it, calling on French architects such as Mathias d'Arras and Italians such as Paolo della Stella. Above the palace which was used as a residence by the exiled Charles X rise the steeples of three churches, including those of the Cathedral of Saint Vitus, which was modeled on the Narbonne Cathedral. Perched on a rock on the banks of the Vltava, like the palace at Cracow, the Royal Palace has dominated the skyline of Czechoslovakia's capital city for centuries.

The Royal Palace, Prague, Czechoslovakia. ▶

Copenhagen, Denmark.

Stockholm, Sweden. ▶

...the legendary phantasmagoria of northern capitals...

Bronze incarnation of Hans Andersen's beloved mermaid princess, heroine of his delightful fairy tale, the Little Mermaid, sitting nonchalantly on her rock, looks out over the harbor of Copenhagen, Denmark's capital since 1167. It was one of the city's bishops, the warrior Absalom, who undertook to make it a commercial center by endowing it with a fortress, on whose site Christianborg Castle stands today. "Kjomandehavn," as the city was then called, soon eclipsed Roskilde, the ancient capital. Today Copenhagen, with its wide avenues and splendid parks, is easily the most smiling and the most relaxed of Europe's big cities.

The last rays of the midnight sun glimmer over Stockholm, dimly illuminating the sheets of ice in Lake Mälar. Legend tells that the blood of a water sprite, killed by the harpoon of a fisherman who was in love with her, mingled with the water of the lake, which, writes Selma Lagerlöf, "shimmered and sparkled and gave off a pink and white luster similar to that found on the inside of a shell." In Riddarholmen, one of the 10,000 islets in the Stockholm archipelago which juts out between Lake Mälar and the Baltic, Birger Jarl in the thirteenth century laid out the foundations of the future capital. At its center, all Swedish kings since Gustavus Adolphus have been laid to rest.

...the heartrending impressionism of a land of fog and gloom...

Westminster Bridge, London, England.

Prey to some of the thickest fogs in the world, London at times can hardly be seen through one of its aptly named "pea-soupers." The Celtic Llyn-Din (Lake Fort), which the Romans changed to Londinium in 43 A.D.—adding the title "Augusta" because of its importance—became in the course of four centuries one of the most prosperous cities in the Roman Empire. Divided into two more-or-less equal parts by the Thames, the intellectual and political capital of Great Britain owes its good fortune above all to its port, used as far back as the Middle Ages by the Hanseatic merchants. London is today Britain's largest port, the second in Europe and the third in the world.

Berne, Switzerland.

Amsterdam, Holland. ▶

...and the passionate life of snow-covered cities.

Covered with a soft blanket of snow, Berne dozes at the witching hour. One of the legends woven about the city tells how, in 1191, Berthold V, Duke of Zähringen, was hunting in the forest through which the River Aare flows, when he was attacked by a huge black bear. After a fierce struggle, the duke managed to plunge his sword into the monster, and, to thank God for saving his life, he built on the very spot a city that was later to be the capital of the Swiss Confederation. The city owes its name to the memory of the bear: "Bär" having become Berne.

Amsterdam, demure daughter of a stormy sea, possesses a special charm in winter, when snow festoons its brick houses. Built entirely on piles, with its canals forming 90 islands linked by more than 400 bridges, the home of the philosopher Spinoza well deserves its nickname of the "Venice of the North." An important commercial center since 1400, it owes its prosperity in part to a strong tradition of tolerance, which during the religious wars made it a generous asylum for persecuted sects, among whose members were many rich foreign families.

MASTERPIECES

OF EUROPEAN ART

BY

EDMOND POGNON

Europe's first face took five centuries to emerge from chaos. From the collapse of the Roman Empire in the West to the age of young Christianity, which took shape as the year 1000 approached, the artist, storm-tossed, dazed, often reduced to a precarious position, does not even seem to be looking for his way. He does not invent. He lets himself be carried along by currents. He cannot continue Greco-Roman humanism: the secrets of the techniques are lost, the lessons of art have dissipated. And even if he could, he would not want to. Even the decaying Roman Empire had deserted academicism, a wizened mummy of the masterpieces of Phidias or Praxiteles, Zeuxis or Parrhasius. It had refreshed itself in deliberate archaism or in those intensely expressive stylizations that are the merit of the Fayum portraits, for example. To this distaste was added, for the now Christian artist of Europe, a general distrust of everything that smacked of paganism. The artist, working almost entirely on churches, had to place himself within the perspectives of a new faith, of a radically different conception of the world. And the sensibilities with which he had to deal were no longer those of the Roman or Romanized élites of the empire's finest days. The new masters were, over the best part of the old empire in the West, barbarians—bearers of an essentially decorative art, of which gold and silverwork, enameling and ornate jewelry had long been fashioned by the nomads of the steppes; in Italy, they were for a time conquerors with Justinian, then they retreated step by step before the Lombards, the generals and exarchs of Byzantium, that vestal virgin of Roman unity. But Byzantium was also a Christian city in Asia, busy expressing, in a plastic language that openly broke with the canons of classicism, its Oriental idea of the supernatural.

And for a long time, far beyond the ephemeral Carolingian restoration, the European artist remakes or imitates. Utensils and religious objects, our only remaining Merovingian artifacts, reveal the traditions and decorative techniques of the barbarians and the nomads of the steppes; the buildings and mosaics of Italy at the time of Justinian are a branch of Byzantine art; in the eighth century the productions of Lombardic Italy, in the ninth century the Carolingian flowering, in the tenth century the Germanic blooming of the three great Ottonian reigns—all these bear witness, through the little we know of their sanctuaries, through the reliefs and mosaics that decorate them, through the illuminations on their manuscripts, through the structure and ornamentation of their objects—to a Byzantine inspiration or to stray impulses toward antiquity redirected by the barbarian temperament.

During the tenth century, whose last decades had seen the Ottonian emperors rally Germany together and sporadically contain Italian anarchy, France had suffered only minor and fruitless disorders. Everything leads us to believe that it had built little—and then mostly in wood—sculpted and painted hardly more. Practically nothing has remained of its fortresses and small churches. France in the year 1000 was a fallow field, a land lain idle for a long time. Yet it needed only less turbulent winds, the sowers less often disturbed, and it would be ready to bear the new harvests of the future more fruitfully than any other land.

The successful establishment of the Capetians, which put an end to a long dynastic conflict, the consolidation of the Duchy of Normandy, the strengthening, in Anjou and Aquitaine, of great families who managed, for better or for worse, to make organized states of their fiefs, quieted the winds a bit. The protection that these experienced princes gave to monastic establishments and at times to episcopal sees gave the sowers a relative calm. And immediately, from the very first years of the eleventh century, France was decked out in that "white mantle of churches" of which the chronicler speaks.

The tyrannical "evolutionism" of our times condemns the art historian to seek out a metamorphosis in every new form. And surely enough, the Romanesque architects did not invent the vaults, already known to Rome and Byzantium, with which they covered their sanctuaries. But the use to which they put them is truly their own. Spaced out, according to the horizontal plan, in bays delimited by the pillars supporting vaults and arcades, ordered in their elevation by the lines of the galleries that back the central cradle vault, Romanesque churches are new solutions to construction problems, original responses to the needs of worship and religious ceremonies, the fruits of an esthetic imagination that scorns precedent.

It is a style that, in those times when the most deeply felt need was for places to house God and worship Him, makes architecture the foremost of the arts. Painting and sculpture are only its handmaidens. And, here again, what tradition could be said to be *continued* by the painted or carved images that in western Europe—while Italy still looks toward Byzantium—abound in the pages of the Apocalypses and sacramentaries where they had been elaborated by intense religious meditation?

Romanesque painters and sculptors certainly studied ivories, cloths embroidered with figures, and even painted manuscripts from the Orient, carried perhaps as far as Spain by the Saracens; here and there they even studied works of the ancients. Their repertory of forms swarms with borrowings. But their art—that they invented.

First, although they had the forms before their eyes, they had nonetheless to reinvent their techniques. In painting, perhaps not; in sculpture, certainly. The sometimes heartrending clumsiness—in which it would be foolish to recognize a deliberate esthetic aim—of so many Romanesque reliefs of the high period bears irrefutable witness to efforts that started from zero. Moreover, in their reliefs as in their frescoes, all the interlacings, stylized palms, and the menagerie of monsters that came to them from the Orient or elsewhere progressively retreat before scenes that are more and more developed, and in which the human figure is increasingly supreme.

There all, or almost all, is new. Composition, always in strict submission to the imperatives of architecture, relegating some Triumph of Christ to the arch of a doorway, winding many a Biblical or hagiographic scene around the tops of pillars, incurvating a whole shortened version of sacred history on the smooth sides of a cradle vault, nonetheless trembles with intense life. Very rarely, when we consider these figures, do we find the solemn immobility of the Byzantine models. Most often, through the accepted or deliberate change in proportions, the summary simplification of anatomy, the stylization of clothing, one encounters real beings that artists saw and looked at. Man's image, with them, is no longer a symbol: it is the seat of thoughts, emotions and movement; for the first time it is a person.

It is now or never that we have to say: Europe, at last. Europe, the civilization of man in movement . . . . But in this Christian West, it is in order to tell the lives of the inhabitants of heaven or the stories in the books dictated by God that Europe is tirelessly fashioned. Whence, in this properly narrative art, the disdain for the individual feature, the refusal of formal realism, the ardent search for the most intense meaning by the accuracy of the gesture, the attitude or the expression of the face. And when by chance it is born in isolation, like those carvings of the Virgin and Child that are hidden away in so many churches, the artist, free of constraint but invested with the same need to give life to a thought, with the same fervor for significance, reaches heights that are sometimes staggering.

The monks, the chief builders of Romanesque churches, immured themselves with their God, contemplated Him in the tabernacle. But for the mass of believers, for whom, from the middle of the twelfth century, larger and larger naves had to be built in towns that were becoming more and more populated, God and His Paradise are in the heavens. Closed, shady and stretching horizontally toward the choir and the dominant altar, Romanesque churches no longer correspond to their naïve faith. Almost overnight, a style in full bloom, and still young, finds itself out of date. And from this same soil of France where it had germinated springs up the entirely new style that the malevolence of the Italians, captivated by classical antiquity, was later to dress up with the name of Gothic.

To raise their vaults high in the air, to pour the light of Heaven into their naves through a thousand colors that articulate its iridescences, this is the ideal of Gothic builders. They then realize that a certain type of vault, called the groined vault, formed by two cradle vaults crossing at right angles according to a square or rectangular plan, exerts its thrust only at the extremities of its two diagonals. They mark or consolidate these diagonals by an ogival transept. Walls are practically no longer needed: pillars, if necessary supported by flying buttresses, are sufficient to bear aloft these light coverings. Immense windows can be opened; and where Romanesque churches could offer only painted walls, Gothic stained-glass windows create colors with light.

There remain, no doubt, surfaces to be painted. But stained glass is continually shrinking them. It is the true painting of the new style—borne along, together with sculpture which maintains or even increases its vitality, in a great revolution of the repertory of forms that is on a par with that of architecture.

People no longer want monsters. They realize that the eminent dignity of man—created in God's image—is offended when his proportions are betrayed and his forms excessively stylized. And so, glowing from the stained glass, leaning on the piers of portraits or on the pillars that, in serried ranks, border them, too triumphant in manner to remain subordinate to structure as Romanesque imagery was, a host of real men and women invade the churches. Celestial or promised to heaven, they must be more serene, more noble and more beautiful than in real life. One example, among a thousand others, is the "Beautiful God" of Amiens. These Europeans are taking again the road formerly explored by the Greeks. But one does not dare reality without risk. Already the Virgin is standing with all her weight on one leg, to balance the weight of the child held in her arm, at whom she is smiling with a tenderness less and less divine; already, set in the patterns of the stained glass or decorating the lower parts of the walls, quadrilobes welcome figures of craftsmen and peasants busying themselves with those "labors of the months" which also illustrate the calendars of the books of hours.

Man, while concerning himself more than ever with his God, takes more and more notice of himself. On tombs, the effigy of the deceased now takes the divinity's place, first engraved, then carved in relief.

The effigy grows more and more lifelike, escapes from the monuments, and becomes a statue. Painting too turns to portraits of living people. The stubborn profile of King Jean painted on a wood panel, now in the Louvre, is succeeded in miniatures by sumptuous manuscripts that are no longer prayer books but book collectors' treasures: those of Charles V and his court. A lay clientele now seeks out the artist, painter, sculptor or architect. The fortress, built of stone beginning in the first half of the eleventh century, is now an enormous and complex citadel, the fruit of a ceaselessly perfected military technique, of which the ruins of the famous Château Gaillard, for example, can still give us some idea. Kings, princes and soon even rich burgesses build themselves town mansions of which too few examples have survived. In countries with a rich municipal life, town halls or "public palaces" stand alongside squares, their façades topped with Flemish belfries or sturdy Tuscan towers. The former calls to mind a bell tower, the latter a donjon; if the North, in fact, is more or less inspired by Gothic sanctuaries in its municipal architecture, the Italian cities, more troubled perhaps by factions, prefer to house the city fathers in buildings whose thick walls and reticent windows make them look like fortresses. Such a one is the Palazzo Vecchio in Florence.

If elsewhere the Gothic movement, born in France —opus francigenum—and in that Norman and Angevin England which was by culture a prolongation of France, soon won over Spain and the countries of the North, Italy rejected it, or almost. It already had made for itself a Romanesque art of its own, strongly favoring Byzantium. It had cultivated painting more than sculpture; under a sky too bright for wide openings, it had kept its walls and almost entirely neglected the art of stained glass. To magnify and vivify smooth and opaque surfaces was what it set out to do.

For a long time Italy had turned to the shores of the Bosphorus for the models of its icons, frescoes and mosaics. Even in the very middle of the thirteenth century a Madonna by Cimabue adds hardly anything to the unmoving majesty of the Theotokos. She is not present in the world of man, she bears him up to heaven. But at the time when the inspired voice of Dante implicates Paradise, Purgatory and Inferno in the most burning human affairs, when believers, meditating on the message of St. Francis, the "poor man" of Assisi, discover that the kingdom of the Beatitudes is, if they want, within their reach, something other than icons is needed.

A Florentine, Giotto, steps in to meet the need. Not that he has the blandness of St. Francis or the bitter violence of Dante, his compatriot—even though he illustrates the works of both these men. To the new needs of human eyes he responds with painting, and only with painting. But what he wants on his wall or panel is to put across the present human form —present to the touch. To suggest the volume, the solidity, more, the weight of the figure, such are the problems, essentially pictorial, that he tries to solve— and is the first man to solve. With his "tactile values," to borrow Berenson's phrase, the third dimension is installed for centuries in European painting—the only painting, observed André Malraux, in which shadows are shown.

While Tuscany undertakes to assimilate Giotto's lesson, with little success for many years, the prosperous Flanders of the great Dukes of Burgundy sees painting undergo innovations of the same order, to which the research of illuminators of manuscripts made a notable contribution. Here it is not so much by the volume of the figures as by the rendering of space that the third dimension is manifested. Another innovation, no less great in consequence: Flemish painting is executed above all on panels, in pictures that are independent of all architecture. And very often, from that time on, these pictures are secular in subject. Two works by Jan van Eyck, the giant of this school, but too soon to fade, fully symbolize these three decisive acquisitions: *The Return of the Mystical Lamb* and *Giovanni Arnolfini and his Wife*. Two very different pictures, one religious, the other secular, but which both attain absolutely convincing effects of depth, the first by a clever setting out of distances, the second by skillful perspective geometry. At the same time the first great Tuscan masters since Giotto are making their appearance. Fra Angelico, who painted only heaven and the saints, would remain the spokesman of an earlier age with his backgrounds of gold and his bright illuminator's palette, if his skill in the composition of scenes and at times in the ordering of planes did not mark him as fully conscious of the new possibilities of his art. Masaccio and Paolo Uccello, his juniors by some twenty years, exploit these new possibilities to the full, and their dissimilar talents add to them still more. The religious painting of the former—who was to die when he was only twenty-seven, well before Fra Angelico—brings into play all the means suggested by the young science of perspective in order to re-create space; his figures, as solid as Giotto's, deck themselves under his brush with an original *morbidezza*. Uccello, for his part, engages boldly in the secular tumult of great battles of soldiers on horseback, the effects of movement, volume and depth that he draws from his subtle geometry, his skillful values and his warm, dark vibrant colors. With them and a few others, in this dawn of the "Quattrocento," the immense revolution started by Giotto is consummated, it reels off its consequences down to the present day. Till then, painting had been content to signify, to give an idea of beings and things. Henceforward it aspires to procure the illusion of these beings and things. A fundamental, and soon a general determination animates all European painters—the determination to let people see. Whoever looks at a painting must feel the same visual sensations as if the artist, instead of covering a flat surface with colors, had had the power really to make his subject surge into space. This space, of which a piece of sculpture can occupy only the limited portion corresponding to its own volume, can hold as much as the painter wants it to on canvas. The whole of the visible world becomes his designated prey. After the primacy of architecture which has marked the Romanesque period, after the hegemony of the Gothic stone figure, painting in Italy now rises fully armed for the imperialist offensive that will make it, perhaps for good, the European art form *par excellence*.

This Italy which, at the same time, was making architecture its own, applied to it too the young creative powers of its awakened genius. And here again, after defending itself for long years against the barbarous example of the "Goths," it is on the attack. With the Florentine Brunelleschi, it finds once more in its Mediterranean and classical tradition a naked beauty that owes virtually nothing to décor, and virtually everything to accuracy of proportions, to simplicity of plan, to a rigorous symmetry and to an exact module of pillars and capitals newly demanded of antiquity. In the very period that sees, in France, Flanders and England, the Gothic style running riot with sinuous feathered arches, and deserving the epithet flamboyant, Brunelleschi tops the Cathedral of Florence by a dome with skillfully incurvated gores; at San Lorenzo he builds a church whose central nave, covered with a paneled ceiling, is decorated only with moldings in two shades of gray and Corinthian capitals and columns—the first Renaissance-style church. He inaugurates, in conceiving the rude and austere Palazzo Pitti, a civil architecture founded on straight lines and solid masses, the essential lesson of which is to reverberate on all the buildings of classical Europe. With Brunelleschi all medieval building arts are doomed.

And certainly, this rejection of facile effects, this voluntary concentration of the creative effort on the essential problems of the harmony of forms could only last a limited time. But while waiting for the baroque reaction to explode, the architectural asceticism of the "Quattrocento" signifies a major departure: to look beautiful an edifice no longer needs works in color or relief. It houses them rather than adorns itself with them. And to the restraint of the Florentine builder is opposed, in violent contrast, the creative exuberance of the painter and sculptor. There are a hundred ways of letting people see, all imperfect and thereby unceasingly challenging the painter to try new methods. But what should the painter let the beholder see? Here, the choice is limitless. He can illustrate, as in the past, the great themes of the Holy Scriptures and the tales of the Golden Legend, or perpetuate the fugitive vision of humble things; fix the features of a living person or confer a sensitive existence to the fables of mythology; bring to life domestic or grandiose scenes, observed, historical or purely imaginary scenes, heavy or not with allegorical meaning . . . . Established on illusion, mute and unmoving, the visible world of painting is still, in one sense, richer than the real world. But in contrast, if it chooses to reflect one of the most everyday aspects, it cannot exhaust it. Each artist exploits a part of it and neglects the rest. There are no two painters who see, cherish and exalt in their works the same vision. A woman's body will captivate the one by the harmony of its forms, another by the suppleness of its postures, and yet another by the tempting radiance or moving fragility of its flesh. The same scene will be, depending on the eye and the heart that have guided the brush, sturdy natural architecture, a paradise of green or a feast of light.

It is henceforward up to each one to choose from among so many manners, varying visions and subjects for painting. And how is one to choose, if not with his own sensitivity? No one knew the names of the carvers of statues at Moissac, Chartres or Strasbourg, or of the illuminators of the vault of Saint Savin's or those at Tavant. But today we know who is responsible for a work. The studio takes second place to the artist, the anonymous group to the person, and style to personality.

But even a genius takes from the surroundings in which he has grown up some of the tendencies that make up his own sensibility. And an artist, in the choice of his subjects, indeed to some extent in his manner, depends on the society for which he produces. But in the use of these common funds, the differences born of the deliberate or spontaneous choice of each artist are henceforward such that beyond geographical and spatial divisions, schools, lineages or temperament make currents that transgress frontiers, and prolong themselves in time.

The common funds of the "Quattrocento": the rebirth of Greco-Roman humanism, destined soon to conquer the whole of Europe. It introduces, side by side with religious subjects called for more than ever by a still opulent Church, mythological themes and, with them, the nude. On the human form that it thus unveils, it imposes the canons of the Ancients. More subtly, it educates the eye to pick out the essential through the accidental, and to guess the secret geometry of each figure. Trends and lessons that favor sculpture make it momentarily fascinating for painters like Mantegna, a devotee of antiquity, whose brush seems to want to rival the effects of the chisel, and procure for it a splendid blossoming with Donatello, Verrocchio (a better sculptor than painter); and finally Michelangelo, a torrent who will in the end overflow the river bed of too-narrow classicism, opening up new ways for the two arts, in both of which he shows himself to be equally sublime.

In these years of apogee, under the infallible ordering of colors and values, thought almost always breaks through. A superabundant thought, irritating because of irritating allusions, behind the exquisite grace of Botticelli's compositions; a serene, relaxed, happy thought beneath the assiduously idealized beauty of Raphael's figures, in the total truth of his portraits; a sovereign thought, mistress of the eye, the senses and the heart, in the *Mona Lisa* —a painting we no longer know how to look at properly—in *St. Anne,* in the *Last Supper* at Milan. Leonardo, who thought of himself almost as a part-time painter, realizes the exact balance, at the highest level, between meaning and optical illusion, between the constraints of the subject and the requirements of composition. After him, it was inevitable that something else had to be invented.

With Michelangelo and Raphael, the artistic center of Italy was displaced. Both, in the company of many others, were called to Rome, where Pope Julius II had just invited the architect Bramante to rebuild Saint Peter's. For a hundred years, work on the basilica will maintain in the metropolis of Christendom an intense creative activity. The edifice, as it rises from the ground, is progressively transformed. Michelangelo, who succeeds Bramante, Raphael, who also cultivates architecture, people the city and its surroundings with churches and palaces in which the lessons of Florence live on only in the art of proportions, while walls garnished with pillars and strongly projecting entablatures have lost their simplicity. There, baroque times are heralded, while at Vicenza Palladio steadily maintains the sober tradition founded by Brunelleschi.

Moreover, a frenzy of building reigns throughout Italy, which is divided between the two trends; throughout France as well, where the companions of Charles VIII, Louis XII and Francis I return dazzled from their campaigns across the Alps. In palaces built by kings and nobles, a superficial Italianism has still not got the better of strong national traditions. The décor calms down, planes become ordered, but the climate maintains the strongly sloped roofs, and towers and turrets are kept. This conflict, once settled, gives birth to a new style, of which the masterpiece is the Château of Chambord.

Painting in France suffers more from the invasion of Italian taste. The great Jean Fouquet had the good fortune to rise to fame before the Italian wars; of transalpine influences he keeps only what he needs to transcend the slow and painstaking efforts of the old illuminators to render volume, space and light. Jean Cousin, under Francis I and Henri II, and with him the whole Fontainebleau school, will have less independence and less success. But sculpture will reward France with Jean Goujon, who, through Roman works, seems truly to have reinvented Greek art.

Although irresistibly drawn toward Italy by all the splendors of the Renaissance, the artists of the northern countries preserved better than in France their national accents. With them the Middle Ages, which had had to cover over very few Roman memories, were taking longer to die. Many, like Lucas Cranach, simply extended them. Of truly new invention, disdainful of Italian influences, one can find German examples only in the abrupt genius, independent of any school, of a Grünewald, whose bloody and tragic *Christ Crucified* in the Karlsruhe museum fully reveals a tortured imagination, a lambent and burning vision, a breathless, grieving touch. In Flanders, Pieter Brueghel's comical, macabre and inexhaustible imagination draws widely even so on the truculence of the soil, in a tradition that Hieronymus Bosch had already illustrated. Dürer, the younger Holbein and Lucas van Leyden listen with passion to the lessons from across the Alps. They gain from them a perfection in drawing and modeling that is never harmed in Dürer by a "rabid precision" inherent perhaps in his Germanic gravity, and which, in Holbein, reigns undivided in portraits raised by their very exactitude to the rank of the greatest European masterpieces.

However, the innovations that Leonardo left others to discover were appearing in Venice. Open to all the winds, kindly, more concerned with pleasure than with thought, the City of the Lagoon had tasted the brilliant Flemish colors as much, through Mantegna's brother-in-law Giovanni Bellini, as the rigor of Florentine forms. From Flanders again, it appears to have learned the recipes for true oil painting, appropriate to a range of effects that was much more varied than the tempera technique practiced in Italy till that time. Born almost at the same time, Giorgione, who died at twenty-three, and Titian, whose long life stretches from one end to the other of the sixteenth century, profit by all these riches. With them, the painter becomes even more of a painter. Without in any way keeping his subject at a distance—even espousing it with a sensuality as yet unknown and which bursts out in his predilection for the female body—he appears to vow to the picture in itself, to the very matter of which he composes it, a wholly new love. A work like Giorgione's *Rustic Concert* is doubly great: it is a poem of natural and carnal beauties, and a symphony of colors and light. In the deeply thought-out portraits, observed and reconstructed at once, that constitute the glory of Titian, the touch, the path of the brush on the canvas can be seen with a sort of hitherto unknown shamelessness, and becomes one of the means that produce the final effects. And on the immense surfaces where soon Tintoretto's rich and bright palette will be lavished, there can be seen an inordinate hunger to paint, which is supported and guided by the two great Venetian initiators.

So in two centuries the two great sources of inspiration of classical art sprang up in Florence and in Venice. While in Bologna the Carraccis undertake to tap them both, and blend them into an eclecticism that only too clearly heralds academicism, other Italians put forward the antithesis and the antidote to them. The antithesis of the classical: that deliberate solicitation of forms which, cultivated in the sixteenth century by Parmigiano, in the sense of grace and elegance is called mannerism; and becomes baroque with the lively sculptures of Bernini who, in Rome, demands from the perilous examples of Michelangelo an exaggerated power of effects. The antidote to academicism: the violent chiaroscuro and the realism, vulgarized by prejudice, of the Neapolitan Caravaggio.

Caravaggio-ism is only a pictorial movement. The baroque is a universal style, in which today's estheticians have even recognized a trend periodically called upon in the history of art to supplant classicism. To take the word only in its strictest sense, baroque is the style that, in the whole of Europe, but in France less than anywhere else, dominated the seventeenth century and the first half of the eighteenth. Versailles is classical by its structures; it is, or rather was, baroque by its interior decoration. In Italy at the same time, and in Rome more than in any other city, churches, façades and monumental fountains are all baroque: complex interplays of curves, striking effects demanded from the distribution of light, from a riot of lively sculpture, from the piling up of make-believe rocks haunted by sometimes strange animals; grandiloquence if you like, but a language that finds a path to the soul and which one must be very petty to challenge.

Built by princes subjugated by the glory of Louis XIV, many palaces and castles in Germany and central

Europe resemble Versailles. But others, and almost all the churches in these countries, turn their backs resolutely on classicism; with their undulating walls, their interior and exterior decoration which calls to mind silverwork and even lacework, they form a properly Germanic branch of the baroque.

Thus "Rococo," encroaching a moment, is to awaken in Italy, around the year 1750, a powerful reaction. A return to antiquity, favored by the increasing discoveries of archaeology, will bring architecture back to simplicity of line and discretion in decoration. France, which under Louis XV had built on the fringe of the baroque current according to the norms of sobriety and harmonious balance, will have no need to do violence to its own feelings to rally to the new canons. The neoclassical buildings that are now to spring up in Europe will be the last ones of traditional architecture to be able to take advantage of a style. The Romantic period, with its taste for the picturesque, will long lead astray, in an amorphous eclecticism, the art of building.

In these full years of the eighteenth century which saw the unleashing of the baroque offensive, one might believe that after the Carraccis, Parmigiano and Caravaggio, all the currents of European painting were henceforward flowing in broad daylight, and that everywhere every artist could tell the line of descendants in which he was situated. It is then that Italy is seen to relinquish the scepter. Already, while in France painters like Le Nain or Georges de la Tour draw lessons from Caravaggio, the Frenchman Poussin—who lives in Rome—surmounts and transcends at the peak of a truly total classicism the threatening academicism of the Carraccis; another Roman by adoption, Le Lorrain, filters through his mists the golden distances of Giorgione. Already in Spain, after El Greco has distilled in the depths of his strange soul, and magnified by his Venetian touch the sinuosities of mannerism, and while Zurbaran, with a Caravaggio-esque chiaroscuro, expresses the cruel and mystic realism of his country, Velásquez, as smitten with his canvas, his palette and his brushes as he is inexorable and impassive before his models, creates the optical illusion of Leonardo da Vinci with the pictorial material of the Titians and Veroneses. Now, at this time, one more country had something new to say, a new country, a part of that Flanders where the pioneers of modern painting had already made themselves known: Holland, recently promoted to its existence as a nation. Protestant and middle-class, it is suspicious of religious, mythological or aristocratic subjects. The real and everyday world is its domain. It exploits it in all its breadth. Thus a school is born, the first in the history of the world, in which portraits, scenes of customs, still lifes and landscapes comprise virtually all painting. It has no

need of distant lessons: the Flemish tradition is already there. All alone, it discovers, with Frans Hals, and his haste to fix as if in flight models that can be at times impatient—like the extraordinary *Gipsy Woman* in the Louvre—what the brush can gain if it does not blur its tracks. And these heirs of the great Flemish primitives, even if they have not looked at Caravaggio's chiaroscuros, would have set out well armed in conquest of that optical illusion (better, *trompe-l'oeil*), which, too mechanical perhaps in Pieter de Hooch, becomes a hallucinating miracle of quiet life with the much more discreet means of the inspired Vermeer. The landscapes of the Ruysdaels and the Van Goyens—the first to be treated for themselves alone, without any subject as a pretext—attain, by the quality of their light, the truth of their big cloudy skies and the depth of their distances, an emotive power hitherto unequaled.

But the Dutchman Rembrandt belongs to no school. He is a whole world. A world seen and rendered with a realism hallowed by his deep and mystical intelligence, a world of portraits and groups and Biblical scenes, a world of light and shade, which is his and his alone.

No painting before him was to this extent the painter himself. Henceforward it is by this total identification of man and work that an artist's greatness will be judged. Watteau, at the beginning of the eighteenth century, when the French school seizes the scepter for a long time, was able to volatilize the academicism codified by Le Brun with a brushwork renewed by Venice; Chardin was able to paint as the French Vermeer; and Fragonard was able to transpose in his luminous vapors and his naughty alcoves a chiaroscuro that owes something to Rembrandt; they are only great—if all three of them are—on this evidence: no other like Watteau, no other like Chardin and no other like Fragonard has conceived, dreamed, felt and seen the world we can see in their paintings.

The "schools" prosper and supply an insatiable demand with a production of excellent quality, thanks to a craft based on the great examples. New ones are even formed, in countries till then more or less absent from the artistic concert, Sweden, England —where only Hogarth, in some of his canvases, manages to free himself from prevailing taste. But it is a force from within that chases Goya from the pleasant, smooth painting of his early years; makes exasperating by his hand the brush of Velásquez, treats his models with a growing ferocity, and alternately pours over his canvases, and the very walls of his house, a world of phantasms whose horror is only the torture of his soul.

In vain David undertakes to depersonalize painting. Ingres is not sustained by his sectarian Raphaelism, but by his singular passion for forms and the almost lecherous sensuality in which his odalisques and goddesses steep themselves. And if his born enemy, Delacroix, engages his mettlesome horses—and his nudes, prostrate or desperately twisted in his massacres—on paths laid out by Rubens, the essential secret of his greatness lies in the last line of his *Diary,* which declares that "The prime merit of a picture is to be a feast for the eyes."

Unheard-of words, which gave satisfaction for the miracles brought about in landscape painting by the Constables, Turners, Boningtons and Corots, and maintained realism on its true level—even though it was that of the powerful Courbet—and prophesied the last metamorphosis of European painting.

For the "isms" can now follow ever more quickly, and even proliferate: they will express only the alibi, quickly abandoned, of the painter who has decided first of all to create a feast for his own eyes. The real world, of which Monet already accepts no more than visual and immediate impressions, can still impose itself on the classical nature of a Manet, win over to its solidity the plastic sentiment of a Renoir, obsess by its mobility the acute vision of a Degas, put to the humble stubbornness of a Cézanne problems that he will think he has never solved, bruise the aching soul of a Van Gogh, send a Gauguin over the seas in search of its simplest aspects, and expose itself to the pitiless clairvoyance of a Toulouse-Lautrec: what all of them want is to paint pictures that they have first seen inside themselves.

And the real world resolved itself in arabesques, in plane geometry or in space, never again to break the surface of a canvas save in an unrecognizable form—and too often scoffed at—the humble servant, or even the useless servant, of the goddess of painting. It only remained for that word to be dismissed altogether. That is what is now being done. Soon there may remain in the picture only that "music" whose presence Delacroix—Delacroix again—was able to discern. "Music," said Gabriel Marcel, "has no meaning: it *is* meaning." Henceforth the same words must be applied to painting, provided it deserves it. And to sculpture as well, since it too aspires to create forms that have no other meaning than themselves.

To mean what they are, such was always the supreme law of forms in architecture; an edifice has never had as its function to represent, but to serve. The beauty of the Greek temple, of the Romanesque or Gothic church, of the Florentine *palazzo* or the Louis Quinze mansion, had no other secret. Even the baroque frenzy expressed, at bottom, a function of the monument: it aimed to put into a certain state the soul of the believer in church, of the courtesan in the palace, and of the city dweller on the pavement of his streets. Forgotten during the long aberrations of the nineteenth-century architects, this law has been rediscovered in our own times. Applied by minds which often see little more than the practical usefulness of the edifice, it seems at times to reduce the building art to a mere technique. But at the same time, this technique, liberated by reinforced concrete and many other advances from the old shackles of weight, lends itself to every boldness. And more than one architect who thinks of himself as a cold realist is a lyrical poet, all the more powerful since he continually seeks to restrain himself.

But the most important thing is perhaps that the architect's mission has entirely changed. He no longer builds palaces for the great men of this world—for whom the old palaces are sufficient. He builds, for all men, factories, ports, railway stations or airports, museums, theaters, churches—though his heart is not always in it—hospitals, but more than anything, houses. There are never enough of them. He has to arrange them in vast units, completely rethink the problems of town planning, aim for economy at the same time as comfort, and sacrifice the superfluous without banishing the amenities. The beauty of these "machines to be lived in" must be born—and in effect is born—from exact adaptation, from strict economy of the means at the architect's disposal, and also from the increasingly "functional" character of the buildings themselves.

People complain a lot about architects. The champions of the past curse their "concentration camp" developments, those who live in these developments are resentful because they have too little room or are too near their neighbors. No one is grateful to architects for leaving the ranks of artists to come to closer grips with their social mission, which has never been so exalting. What would be said of the architect if, envying the glory of the painter or sculptor, he aspired to deliver his personal and unique "message" without thinking of those who were to receive that message?

E. P.

The choice of the most evocative masterpieces of European art, presented in this chapter, was made after a widespread inquiry among the curators and directors of the great museums of Europe. In particular we would like to thank Dr. A. van Schendel, Director General of the Rijksmuseum, Amsterdam; M. René Berger, Director and Curator of the Musée Cantonal des Beaux-Arts, Lausanne; Sr. Manuel Lorente, Assistant Director of the Museo del Prado, Madrid; Mr. Eivind S. Engelstad, Director of the Kunstindustri Museet, Oslo; Professor Huggler, Director of the Berner Kunstmuseum, and Dr. Peter Krieger, of the Berlin Staatlichen Museum, for their very kind cooperation.

Poussin: "The Ashes of Phocion," Paris, France.

Twenty centuries after Pericles,

the Greek miracle fleshed out

the dreams of a great European

painter. But meanwhile...

Classicism's sovereign order dominates all the work of Nicolas Poussin, for whom painting was a "function of reason." "Perhaps with no other artist has the head so dominated the craft," wrote André Gide, who greatly admired the painter. Norman by birth (1594), taciturn and a homebody, Poussin went to live in Rome when the baroque period was at its peak. He loved the city for its ruins, and he quickly made a name for himself there as one of the most successful artists of the day. He left Italy only once, in 1640—and even then he returned as quickly as he could—at the repeated instance of Louis XIII, in order to direct official painting in France. In 1648 he completed "The Ashes of Phocion," a painting which was intended to be paired with "The Obsequies of Phocion." The two canvases are inspired by the story, attributed to Plutarch, of a fourth-century B.C. Athenian general who was unjustly condemned for treason, then rehabilitated posthumously.

Cornerstone of Western civilization, the Parthenon, a place of pilgrimage for all the great minds of Europe, is the most perfect expression of classical balance and the most admirable reflection of that stable world in which the Greeks briefly thought —the moment of the "Greek miracle"—that they could arrest the march of time. The history of the edifice goes back to the sixth century B.C., a time when Athens wanted to offer a new temple to its protectress, Pallas Athena. Two projects were begun, the Pericles initiative won the day and, in 447 B.C., work on a Parthenon in Pentelic marble began, under the direction of the sculptor Phidias. Work continued for fifteen years. Up until the fourth century, the name "parthenon" (chamber of the virgins) designated only one of the rooms in the building which, according to inscriptions, was known over-all as the "great temple." Intended by its builders as a sanctuary, it came to be considered by the Athenians more as an artistic masterpiece, one of the republic's treasures, than as a sacred place.

The Parthenon, Athens, Greece. ▶

Tympanum of the Church of St. Pierre, Moissac, France.

...how endless and various the quest! Europe saw the arch and the vault dominate the Andalusian mosque of the ninth century as they did the Aquitanian church of the eleventh...

A gospel in stone, the tympanum at Moissac (twelfth century) handsomely presents the apocalyptic vision, a decorative theme frequently used on religious buildings in the Romanesque period. Adorning the façade of the Church of Saint Pierre (fifteenth century), it has survived undamaged, as have the figures on the supporting columns. The eyes of the four Evangelists and the twenty-four old men of the Apocalypse converge on Christ, the axis of the entire composition, which rests on a lintel of white Pyrenean marble decorated with rosettes. The multifoil jambs exhibit the influence of Hispano-Moorish art as a result of the sanctuary's privileged position on the pilgrims' road to Santiago de Compostela.

A forest of many-colored precious pillars, the Great Mosque at Córdoba is supported by 850 sandstone, jasper, green or violet breccia marble columns which were gathered from the four corners of the earth. During one of Europe's most splendiferous periods, Abd-er-Rahman I decided to build a mosque for his capital which would surpass all others in its grandeur and magnificence. Begun between 785 and 788, it was enlarged by each of the Arab sovereign's successors until the end of the tenth century. When Córdoba was reconquered from the Moors by King (later Saint) Ferdinand, in 1236, the mosque was converted into a cathedral simply by closing the ends of the nineteen naves opening on the patio, and purging the sanctuary, which was henceforth dedicated to the Assumption of the Virgin.

◀ The mosque at Córdoba, Spain.

Akin to sculpture in its strength, Giotto's paintings exhibit a relief which, even if it has not yet developed into the perspective of the Renaissance, still heralds it and prepares the way for it. Giotto (1266-1337) was one of those who, with Cimabue, wrested painting from the two-dimensional tradition of Byzantine art by basing their work on Gothic statuary, as André Malraux has observed. Once a shepherd—or so tradition holds—he possessed a well-developed sense of composition and did much to make painting of his day more human then ever before. In his work, Élie Faure remarks, "there trembles something of which the Greeks knew nothing, the sorrow around the mouths, the gentleness in the eyes, the confidence that man momentarily had in man." The splendid "Madonna Enthroned," which Giotto painted about 1310, is today one of the most important pieces in the Uffizi Gallery in Florence.

◄ Giotto: "Madonna Enthroned," Florence, Italy.

saw painting

steal the third

dimension

from sculpture...

The faith of the Middle Ages lives on in this austere Romanesque Virgin, carved some time between the tenth and thirteenth centuries, that period of exceptional artistic fecundity experienced throughout the Christian West, but above all in France. It was a period of peace —with the Norman invasions ended—and economic progress, during which the devout expressed the spontaneous intensity of their faith with an ardor unique in the history of Christianity. In the smallest, most distant parishes in Auvergne, countless religious buildings sprang up; their ornamentation celebrating the popular wonder in the face of great divine works. The Mother of Christ, "the Lady clothed in sun," especially is celebrated as the Mediatrix by many "Seated Virgins"; but the finest of these is undoubtedly the carving of Our Lady of Saint Gervasy, which illuminates a small Romanesque church in Puy-de-Dôme with its serene grandeur.

Our Lady of St. Gervasy, France.

...saw the face of man, studied in life or meditated in Scripture, reveal the inner soul...

The anguish of an epoch torn between the Middle Ages and the Renaissance is visible in the work of the great artist Albrecht Dürer (1471-1528) who, despite two trips to Venice where he came to know Bellini, was deeply marked, as his engravings bear witness, by the atmosphere of medieval superstition still prevalent in a Germany which Luther was about to cast into turmoil. Dürer, with a persistence that heralds Rembrandt or Van Gogh, examined his face clinically, almost psychoanalytically. In the self portraits which he began doing when he was thirteen—the one in the Louvre was done when he was twenty-two—one can discern the doubts characteristic of all those who witness the dawning of a new world, but also, at the same time, a basic affirmation of the individuality of every man.

◀ Dürer: Self portrait, Paris.

One of the most beautiful works of the early Renaissance, Donatello's "John the Baptist" exhibits a rarely equaled technical proficiency. Born in Florence in 1386, apprenticed to Ghiberti—he helped with the work on the bronze doors of the Baptistery—Donatello was not only a sculptor, but also a member of the painters' guild, an architect and an engineer. Due to his sense of the dramatic and the tragic, he stands out clearly in his age, the age of Della Robbia and Verrocchio. Donatello created a large body of work which deeply influenced Michelangelo, then Rodin, who considered him his master. And although his first years unfolded at the end of the Gothic Age, he died in 1466 at the height of the Renaissance. His marble statue of John the Baptist, carved in 1440, can be seen today in the Palazzo Bargello in Florence.

Donatello: "John the Baptist," ▶ Florence, Italy.

Nervi : Grand Palace of Sports, Rome, Italy.

...and saw the Gothic arch, still at the heart of functional architecture in its mathematical rigor, developed, refined, and complicated.

To give concrete a soul, to free modern materials of their dullness and return to them the elegance of the Gothic Age that he so admires, this is the aim of the great Italian architect Nervi. "As often as possible," he declared, "I go and revivify myself at the best possible sources: medieval cathedrals." Pier Luigi Nervi, who likes to think of himself more as a technician than an artist, has created magnificent modern structures with soaring arches and spacious vaulted ceilings. Among his works are the Grand Palace of Sports that was built for the 1960 Olympic Games in Rome, the famous exhibition halls in Turin, an elevated highway in Rome, the tallest skyscraper in Europe—Milan's Pirelli Building—and even concrete hulls for World War II freighters.

Like hands joined in prayer, the pillars of Lincoln Cathedral perfectly express the divine call of Gothic art: to express the purified ardor of a spirituality striving heavenward. Situated on a hill, it looks down on one of the oldest of English cities. As early as 1090, a primitive Norman-style church founded by William Rufus stood on this site. The first church was destroyed by fire in 1141, and only a few traces of it can be discovered in the present edifice, begun in the reign of Henry II, who was crowned there in 1158. The extension behind the main altar of the cathedral was added between 1255 and 1280, while the towers, one 200, the other over 260 feet high, were rebuilt in the fourteenth century.

◀ Lincoln Cathedral, England.

In Florence,
the most disturbing
of painters seems
to exaggerate
the folds
of a Hellenistic
Victory he has
never seen...

To affirm the glory of mankind was the ultimate aim of Greek art, from the first "kouroi" until the Hellenistic world went into decline. It is an ambition that is plainly visible in the "Victory of Samothrace." A magnificent marble figure dating from the second century B.C., the "Victory" was discovered in 1863 on the island of Samothrace, in the Aegean Sea, by Champoiseau, a member of a French mission. Set on the prow of a galley, it would appear to commemorate some sort of victory by the fleet of Rhodes. The finding of one of its hands in 1950 suggests that its outstretched arm was making a gesture of victory. It is today the most famous piece of Hellenistic sculpture in the Louvre, where it adorns a landing.

◀"Victory of Samothrace," Paris, France.

The mannerism of Botticelli's paintings with their distortion of scale, perspective and lighting effect within a formal framework, anticipate modern art. Born in 1444, Botticelli lived in the refined Florence of Lorenzo the Magnificent, amid the pomp and among the most brilliant minds of the Renaissance. A great reader, an admirer of Plato and the illustrator of Boccaccio, he boldly expressed the paganism of his times for much of his life. But in his middle years, the influence of Savonarola converted him to an impassioned Christianity. Beginning in 1494 he abandoned mythological subjects and began to illustrate the Gospels. The "Allegory of Spring," exhibited in the Uffizi, in Florence, is one of his earlier masterpieces, having been executed in 1477 or 1478 for the Villa di Castello.

Botticelli: "Allegory of Spring," Florence, Italy. ▶

...while a living woman inspires Leonardo to an absolute masterpiece.

The fantastic exuberances of a powerful Flemish painter...

The divergent forces shaping Flemish painting are plainly visible in the work of Brueghel, torn between the serenity of "primitive" painting which a century earlier had expressed man's adaptation to his times, and the political and religious conflicts of his own age, which were in turn accentuated by the triumph of the Renaissance throughout Europe. Hence Brueghel's bizarre mixture of secular, peasant, mythological and mystic subjects. The latter especially are treated, not after the quiet manner of a Van Eyck or a Memling, but with a frenzy which echoes the deviltries of Hieronymus Bosch. Brueghel was born some time between 1520 and 1530. He painted his "Tower of Babel," whose architecture was inspired by Rome's Colosseum and Imperial Baths, in 1563. The painting is now in the Boymans Museum in Rotterdam.

Brueghel: "The Tower of Babel," Rotterdam, Holland.

The most beautiful woman in the world, as well as the most famous and the most mysterious, the "Mona Lisa" has probably had more written about it than any other art object in all history. Its lifelikeness amazed Vasari: "The mouth, which the redness of the lips blends into the flesh tints of the face. . . it is no longer color, it is truly flesh. In the hollow of the neck, a careful observer might catch the pulsing of the artery...." The intense life and luminous brightness of the face radiate from eyes which seem truly to return the gaze of the spectator. Only Stendhal seems to have escaped Mona Lisa's spell: "It is surprising," he wrote, "that this pretty woman has no eyebrows." Mona Lisa stands against an unusual misty scenic setting, bathed in an unreal twilight glow, which calls to mind the landscapes of Chinese paintings.

Leonardo da Vinci: "Mona Lisa," Paris, France. ▶

...which bear little resemblance to the calculated profundities of his great ancestor, provide a distant accompaniment to the contained lyricism of the architects of Touraine.

◀ Van Eyck: "Giovanni Arnolfini and his Wife," London.   Chambord, France.

To give style to royalty by this royalty of a style was the aim of Francis I of France when he undertook to build Chambord in 1519. On the banks of the Loire, this magnificent château lifts its famous forest of chimneys and bell turrets above walls imbued with classic serenity. A perfect illustration of the French Renaissance, it was built by the architects Neveu and Sourdeau according to plans by Domenico di Cortona. In 1821 it was given to the Duke of Bordeaux, Count of Chambord, by national subscription ; the property of the Bourbon-Parmas since 1886, it was acquired by the State in 1932.

The perfection of his realistic style (he paid greater attention to detail than perhaps any other painter in the entire history of painting) helped to establish the reputation of Jan van Eyck (1390-1444) during his lifetime. By the precision of his lines, by emphasizing the severity of an object, by the extraordinary brilliancy of his colors, Jan van Eyck so disrupted contemporary painting that art historians now speak of an "Eyckian revolution." Another cause of this revolution was the care Van Eyck took to express the individual personality of his models with an acuteness that is quite modern, as can be clearly seen in the portrait of the banker Arnolfini and his wife. Van Eyck's influence was considerable ; his manner and his technique with oils spread throughout Europe, affecting among others the Italian Antonello da Messina, and the German Cranach.

Venus de Milo, Paris, France.

With its almost human statues, Greek sculpture of the decadence displays a realism that denies transcendency, and has eliminated all evidence of the spiritual element which still distinguished Greek art three centuries earlier, in the archaic period. Naturalistic, emotional, sometimes even theatrical, Hellenistic art has however given us in the "Venus de Milo" a masterpiece of unsurpassed majesty. The statue has long been thought to date from the fourth century B.C., but certain details of the technique, such as the arrangement and workmanship of the drapery and the hair, suggest the sculptor may have lived as late as the second century B.C. The Venus was discovered in 1820 at Milo, a small island in the Cyclades, following a search undertaken at the suggestion of the explorer Dumont d'Urville.

In those times Venus
was restored to her throne: royal painters
put her on canvas...

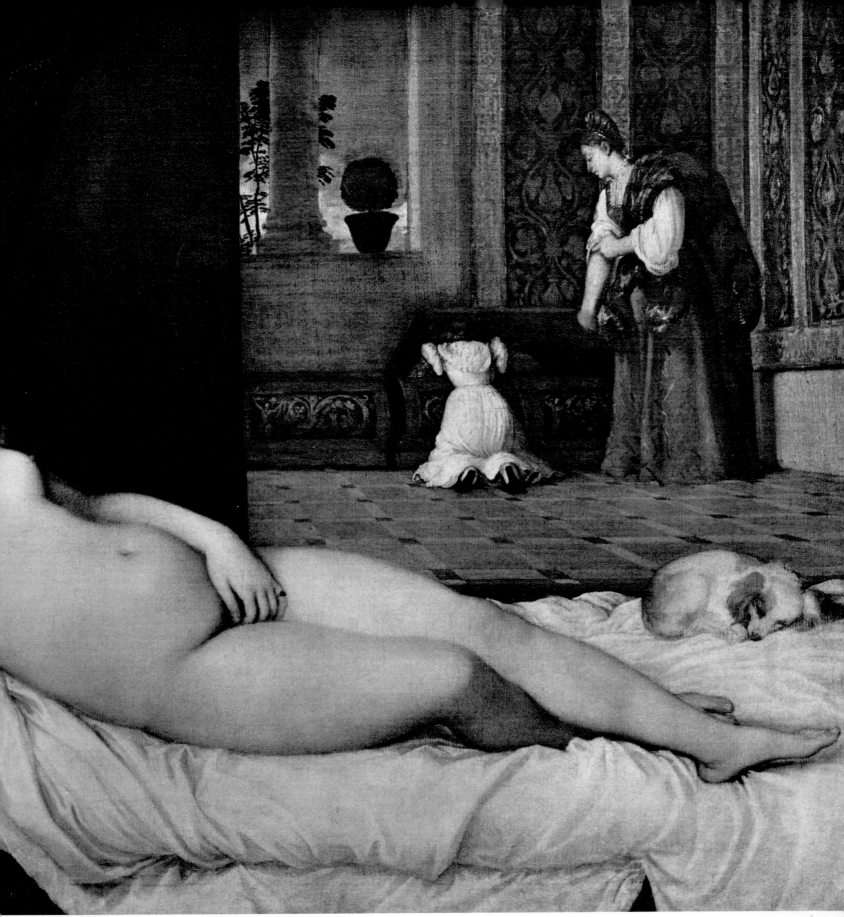

Venus of Urbino, Titian, Florence, Italy.

The wave of sensuality that arose in Venice in the sixteenth century, even as the Most Serene Republic began on the course of slow decline which would reach its critical climax two centuries later, found its most brilliant master in the great Titian (1477-1576) whose "Bacchanalia," "Danae" and "Offerings to Love" today hang in the great museums of Europe. Then there is the "Venus of Urbino," now in the Uffizi, in Florence, which was part of the Della Rovere inheritance. Painted in 1538 for Duke Guidobaldo II, it is one of the finest works of the artist's maturity. Titian reigned over the Golden Age of Venice for more than sixty years, ending his life in painful meditation on the Passion of Christ, even while at the same time painting several canvases which modern criticism considers as heralding the Impressionist masters.

...but an unleashed creativity went on to prophets hewn from marble, and to cupolas raised to the glory of the true God...

Like a lonely Titan, Michelangelo's "Moses" mounts guard above the tomb of the warrior pope Julius II in the Church of San Pietro in Vincoli. The first grandiose project of the sculptor was abandoned after he had begun work, and only one of the six monumental statues originally planned, "Moses" (1542), was set up on the Roman mausoleum. Six "slaves" were also started, but only two were finished—these today are in the Louvre, in Paris. The other four still remain unfinished, just as the master left them—only partly emerged from their blocks of stone—and can be seen in the Accademia in Florence. By the breadth of his genius, which places him in the first rank of painters as well as of sculptors and architects, Michelangelo Buonarroti (1475-1564), in turn considered the "greatest of the Gothics" by Rodin and a "decadent Romantic" by Bourdelle, is, along with Leonardo da Vinci, the most notable artist produced by sixteenth-century Italy.

Michelangelo: "Moses," Rome, Italy. ▶

To improve on the empiricism of the medieval builders, to create an architecture in which mathematical calculations would support and channel creative intuition, was the ambition of the humanist architects of the "Quattrocento," of whom Brunelleschi (1377-1446)—who drew the plans of the famous cathedral at Florence—was the most outstanding. A Florentine by birth, he traveled to Rome and returned with a fervent admiration of antiquity and the ancients' natural equilibrium, which he proceeded to emulate in his own buildings. Brunelleschi was one of those Renaissance men who by their genius imposed the idea of individual talent and transformed architecture, formerly a collective expression, into a personal one.

Brunelleschi: Dome, Florence, Italy. ▶▶

◀ Tintoretto: "Crucifixion" (detail), Venice, Italy.

Bernini: "St. Theresa in Ecstasy" (detail), Rome, Italy.

...and to tumultuous visions of His Passion, or the faces of saints swooning for love of Him.

Tintoretto's tumultuous talent fills the walls of the Scuola San Rocco, which is completely devoted to his works and where the indefatigable Venetian master, who strove to reconcile "Michelangelo's drawing and Titian's brushwork," covered hundreds of square yards of canvas with his paintings, of which his "Crucifixion" is the undenied masterpiece. It required only a year, 1565, for the painter to execute this huge picture crowded with dozens of figures. Jacopo Robusti (1518-1594) was born in Venice, the son of a dyer, whence the nickname Tintoretto—it means "little dyer"—by which he is known today. It was from his great works that first Rubens, then Delacroix drew a great part of their inspiration.

A secular ecstasy seems to take possession of the holy figures of Bernini (1598-1680), who strongly influenced all sixteenth-century Italian baroque, and is responsible for many of the Roman monuments which can still be admired today. The man who was called "Cavaliere Bernini" was gifted with extraordinary ability. A sculptor, but also an architect and a painter, he was capable of undertaking the most varied tasks—a fountain, a church façade, a statue of David, or the colonnade of Saint Peter's. The face of "St. Theresa in Ecstasy" admirably expresses the mixture of sweetness and suffering that she claimed to have felt when the angel pierced her heart with the arrow of divine love.

Rembrandt: "The Pilgrims of Emmaus," Paris, France.

Vézelay Basilica, France. ▶

Rembrandt, whose chiaroscuro seems filtered through medieval vaults.

Christian spirituality literally radiates from the famous "Pilgrims of Emmaus" (1648). "The keen ardor of this face, which is made evident not by the over-all picture but which derives rather from the set of the lips and the expression," wrote Eugène Fromentin in his "Masters of Past Times," "is priceless ; no art can duplicate this, no one before Rembrandt, and no one since him has expressed it as well." The master of chiaroscuro was born in Leyden in 1606. Famous by the time he was twenty-five, Rembrandt died in 1669, hounded by his creditors, forced from one lodging to another, abandoned and alone. No man has ever searched the decadence of his own face with more lucidity than Rembrandt, in his famous series of self-portraits.

As solemn and pure as a hymn, the nave of the basilica at Vézelay raises its well-known curved outline against a background of the Burgundy landscape which conceals so many Romanesque treasures. The edifice was built in honor of St. Madeleine between 1120 and 1135, on the ruins of an abbey founded in 864. The little town, where St. Bernard preached the Second Crusade in 1147, was then a prosperous place of pilgrimage, and its fairs were equal in fame to those of Troyes or Beaucaire. But in the thirteenth century doubts were cast on the authenticity of the relics of St. Madeleine, which had long been objects of pious veneration, and the ensuing skepticism brought an end to the pilgrimages, which also destroyed Vézelay's prosperity.

Christ. Stained-glass window in the Church of Our Lady at Madley, England.

El Greco: "The Burial of the Count of Orgaz," Toledo, Spain.

A profound faith informed El Greco, whose faces are seen again in Gothic stained glass.

The colorful splendor of medieval stained glass is excellently illustrated in the so-called "primitive" works of the twelfth and thirteenth centuries in Great Britain. Stained glass originally answered two needs: to admit light and to teach religious history to the faithful, the majority of whom were illiterate. A catechism of the period contains the following question and answer: "What must we do when we enter a church? — We must take the holy water, worship the Holy Sacrament, then walk around the church and look at the stained-glass windows." This head of Christ, which adorns the east bay of the Church of Our Lady at Madley, in Herefordshire, dates in all probability from the twelfth century.

The fervor of a living flame burns in all El Greco's painting, and especially in his masterpiece, "The Burial of the Count of Orgaz" (1584), which adorns the Church of Santo Tomé at Toledo. Domenico Teotocopulo, known as El Greco ("The Greek") was born some time between 1545 and 1550 at Candia, on the island of Crete. He began his career as a painter in Italy where he was exposed to the influence of Tintoretto. About 1575, El Greco turned toward Spain, and was an accomplished painter by the time he settled in Toledo where he spent the remainder of his life, a respected artist. His work, however, was largely unknown until the nineteenth century, although today El Greco is considered to be the most illustrious herald of Expressionism.

Mystics of daily life are the Dutchman Vermeer

and, later, the Frenchman Chardin, both bourgeois...

To catch eternity in his canvases was the aim of Vermeer, whose work long remained unrecognized and all but unknown, confused with that of the lesser masters of his day to the extent that some of his paintings were bought as works by Maes or Metsu. A Dutchman, born in Delft in 1632, Vermeer, whom Marcel Proust considered the greatest painter of all time, died in 1675 at forty-three, leaving behind some forty paintings, one of which is this marvelous "Lacemaker" which was sold as recently as 1870 for the equivalent of $600 or £215, and is today literally priceless.

"It is possible to create a masterpiece with a jug and some fruit," said Jean-Baptiste-Siméon Chardin, poet par excellence of everyday things and domestic objects, which he painted with patience and a refreshing lack of pretentiousness. "No one in France can compare with him from the death of Watteau to the Revolution," wrote André Malraux. Born in Paris in 1699, Chardin seems to have been a man with no social ambitions, a man who placed his home first and foremost, enjoyed no contacts with the court and was little known by contemporary artists and critics.

◀ Vermeer: "The Lacemaker," Paris, France.

Chardin: "The Smoking Room," Paris, France.

Forerunner of the "Sturm und Drang" which was to sweep Germany, a breath of baroque moves through the sumptuous Residenz at Würzburg, which is responsible for both the charm and the notoriety of the capital city of Lower Franconia. It was the initiative of the bishop-princes Franz and Karl von Schönborn which was responsible for the building of the Residenz in the years between 1720 and 1740, by Balthasar Neumann. The architect's skill is especially visible in the monumental staircase (1742), the brilliant decoration of which was executed by Giovanni Battista Tiepolo. Above the twin flights of stairs and the vast landing, Tiepolo's ceiling is a symphony of colors, arranged in four compositions; the figures, borne upward in an irresistible surge of fanfare and cloud, symbolize the four continents. Paying homage to the genius of Neumann, the painter showed the architect, in a colonel's uniform, seated on a cannon, while his own portrait on a medallion hangs above Europe.

...but for the princes,
even those of the Church,
outsize palaces were needed...

The Residenz, Würzburg, Germany. ▶

The reflection of an overweening pride, the architecture of the Palace of Versailles marks the triumph of classicism, which is such a strong component of the French temperament. Originally, the most famous palace in the world was but a humble hunting lodge, the ''card castle,'' built in 1631 during the reign of Louis XIII. In 1661, Louis XIV, the Sun King, limited himself to prettifying it by the addition of splendid gardens by Le Nôtre. But since the actual dwelling was too small, lordly rather than regal, Le Vaux undertook a ''second Versailles'' in 1668. He enveloped the original brick-and-stone palace with parallel buildings and pavilions which he decorated with terraces whose horizontal lines extended Le Nôtre's already wide perspectives. In 1679, Mansart, succeeding to the direction of the works, built the Hall of Mirrors and the two huge wings which frame the main building of the palace. Its arrogant proportions give the whole building a feeling of imposing majesty.

...whether their taste
was classical or inclined
toward the baroque...

The Palace of Versailles, France.

Melk Abbey, Austria.

The triumphal prow of baroque art, the Abbey of Melk, set on a rock almost 200 feet high, proudly commands the Danube.   Paul Claudel wrote of this glorious style, which came from Italy to conquer all of Europe, "It no longer presents a tragic view of Christianity, but rather one at once triumphant and yet merciful, that is in harmony with the most profound and most noble needs and aspirations of human nature." Melk owes its beauty to the genius of the German architect, J. Prandtauer, who rebuilt it in the eighteenth century on the ruins of an ancient edifice of unknown origin.   Some Benedictines had been settled there by the Margrave Leopold II in 1089.   During the reign of Leopold III the monastery became independent and soon gained an importance that made it one of the wealthiest of Austrian abbeys.   Then it fell into a decline which continued from the twelfth to the seventeenth centuries.   Melk, occupied by the French army in 1805 and 1809, was twice used by Napoleon as his headquarters.

Games of love furnished inspiration for Watteau, who, like Mozart, laid a veil of melancholy over his work almost as if to herald his premature death.   Indeed, he died at thirty-seven, already made famous by his talent; "The Embarkation for Cythera" (in the Louvre) is his masterpiece.   Here, refined inspiration is well served by an astonishingly delicate technique, in the slightly sad vision of a transient but precious happiness.   Watteau (1684-1721), born at Valenciennes, was a roofer's son.   Despite his humble origins, it was he who handed down to posterity the image of Parisian aristocracy, into which he was introduced by Crozat, the collector of Venetian paintings, who invited him to musical soirées attended by the most beautiful women of Parisian society and which were to be his lifelong inspiration.

Watteau: "The Embarkation for Cythera," Paris, France.   ▶

...when Watteau embarked his pilgrims to Cythera in the skiffs of his dream.   Graces forgotten...

Rodin: "The Gate of Hell," Paris, France.

...when Romanticism came to exaggerate beauty through horror, and later when the chisel of a genius made thought quiver in the body of a Hercules.

A Promethean strength fills the sculptures of Auguste Rodin, all of whose work is marked with a sense of dramatic tension unparalleled since Michelangelo. Schooled at the École des Arts Décoratifs, Rodin (1840-1917) was forty before he executed his first works: "The Age of Iron" and "John the Baptist," whose virtuosity literally stunned the art world. "The Thinker"—above, the version atop Paris' Porte de l'Enfer, the "Gate of Hell"—is a work of the artist's mature years in which life is expressed without the slightest irrelevant line, and with a force that has made the sculpture a symbol of inner concentration throughout the world.

Order in chaos, Romantic frenzy restrained by a powerful sense of synthesis and composition—those are the characteristics of Eugène Delacroix's genius. At twenty-four he wrote: "Let us work calmly and without haste.... As soon as I begin to perspire and my blood to run hot, beware. Slipshod painting is the painting of a slipshod man." Born at Saint-Maurice in 1798, he is said to have been the diplomat Talleyrand's illegitimate son. The greatest of the French Romantic painters was also a very cultured man who had read Shakespeare, Dante, Ariosto and especially Byron, from whom he borrowed the subject of "The Death of Sardanapalus" in 1827. This picture is one of the artist's finest works. The last page of his "Diary" bears this sentence: "The prime merit of a picture is to be a feast for the eyes."

Delacroix: "The Death of Sardanapalus," Paris, France. ▶

Hogarth: "The Shrimp Girl," London, England.

The merry Hogarth was far off then,

and the court of Spain fell victim

to a fierce painter, who...

"Be observant in the streets, the gardens, the markets, in the houses, and then you will acquire an accurate idea of what movement really is in life's activities," wrote Diderot in his "Essay on Painting," and it is as if in response to his contemporary's precept that Hogarth (1697-1764) throughout his life studied the ordinary men and women of England, whose daily lives he not merely painted, but literally engraved. His "Shrimp Girl" is today one of the most important works owned by the National Gallery in London. Hogarth's talent as a satirist was not greatly appreciated by the high society of his day, who were only beginning to enthuse over the "grand manner" of Reynolds and Benjamin West.

Goya turned a merciless gaze on the great men of his day, uncompromisingly describing their moral blemishes and their physiological degeneration. In his "Carlos IV and His Family," the painter had no hesitation about showing himself, in the words of Eugénio d'Ors, as a "circus animal trainer behind his docile troupe." A masterpiece of irreverence, this picture at the same time reveals his prodigious talent for using color: "Where are lines found in nature?" asked Goya. "I myself can only distinguish bright-colored bodies on the one hand and dark ones on the other." Born at Fuendetodos in 1746, the son of a gilder, Goya also produced a number of hallucinatory etchings that are among the masterpieces of the history of engraving. At the end of his life, troubled by deafness, he was to branch out as a visionary artist, populating his canvases with monsters and witches. It is Manet whose work most exhibits the influence of the man whom Baudelaire counted as one of the beacons of humanity.

◀ Goya: "Carlos IV and His Family," Madrid, Spain.

Renoir: "Le Moulin de la Galette," Paris, France.

...like his illustrious predecessor, spared only the children. But art cannot long forget joy:

Renoir the tender, much of whose work was devoted to the exaltation of woman and to the ordinary joys of life, was thirty-five when he painted the "Moulin de la Galette," which exhibits clear evidence of the artist's maturity as well as of his sharp sense of color. Renoir was then under the influence of Impressionism, which later he gradually abandoned in favor of a more traditional, more carefully composed art, which would ultimately, toward the end of his life, even lead him into sculpture. At the age of thirteen he was already earning a living by painting chinaware, from which he acquired his taste for bright clear colors. When his family settled in Paris he came with them and went to work in Gabriel-Charles Gleyre's studio, where he came to know Bazille, Monet and Sisley. In his last paintings there is not the least sign of the agony he suffered in order to paint when, around 1900, sciatica paralyzed his hands and he was forced to employ the device of having his brush tied to his wrist.

Imperturbable and inflexible to his models, Velásquez managed to combine the pictorial matter of a Titian or a Veronese with the visual effects of a Leonardo da Vinci. He was gifted in his ability to capture all the minute variations of light, down to the least scintillation. Among his numerous portraits of the great, that of "Las Meniñas" (on the facing page is the central detail, the Infanta María Margarita) is undeniably his masterpiece. If his early canvases are distinguished by their strong relief, in his later work he abandoned the outlines of objects and diffused solid form into spots of color, ignoring details in order to achieve an over-all impression of nature and of light particles as they strike the eye, thus making himself one of the fathers of Impressionism.

◀ Velásquez: "Las Meniñas," Madrid, Spain.

Van Gogh: "Man with a Severed Ear," London, England.

...if the joy of baroque Flanders found no echo in the soul of the man with the severed ear, it found echoes in any number of its own paintings...

In strident conflict, colors explode with an emotional impact. The "Portrait of a Man with a Severed Ear" was painted on January 21, 1899, in the Yellow House at Arles ; less than three months earlier, in the heat of a quarrel with Gauguin, Van Gogh had sliced off part of his ear with a razor. Searching for a reality illuminated by a sense of inner excitement, for a realism of expression rather than of style, Van Gogh reached the point where he was obsessed by a true symbolism of color. Ultramarine blue meant the infinite to him, red and green were "dreadful human passions."

A whirlwind frenzy which achieves magnificent balance, Rubens' "The Village Fair" was supposedly painted in a single day. The master, it is true, worked with a team. Concerned more here with a realism of expression than with subservience to the Flemish baroque style, of which he was the creator, he imagined odd deformations, grimacing masks and all sorts of pathetic positionings, which often express, as they do here, complete drunken abandon. The country festival becomes an apocalypse. The generous nature of the painter, Flemish by race as well as by temperament, prescribed strong characters: the women are plump and sensual, all but bursting with health, the men broad-chested, vigorous and hearty, with bulging muscles.

Rubens: "The Village Fair," Paris, France. ▶

Le Corbusier: Monastery of La Tourette, France.

...some who build can create it with light,

and some who paint in restless

anxiety create it in full radiance.

To obtain an "unrestrained expression of feeling by the interplay of proportions," thus Le Corbusier, the greatest living architect, defined his intent when he created, between 1956 and 1959, the Monastery of Sainte-Marie de La Tourette, which marks the culmination of his life's work. "I conceived the forms, contacts and circuits required so that prayer, liturgy, meditation and study might come naturally in this house," explained the artist whose style, marked by restraint as well as by a sense of strength, metamorphized rough concrete, and brought a plastic strength that is eminently modern to this heretofore austere and unfeeling material. Situated at Évreux-sur-Arbresle, the Monastery of La Tourette was intended to house young Dominicans from Lyons during their first years in the Order; it contains a hundred rooms.

"I wanted to make something solid and lasting out of Impressionism," said Cézanne (1839-1906) seeking to point out what distinguished the intent of his paintings from those of a Pissarro or a Monet. But if he wanted to portray shapes and display the weight and materiality of objects, he sought to do so without the assistance of drawing: color alone should suffice to shape contours. This approach is particularly well illustrated by his "Mont Sainte-Victoire and the Black Castle," and it characterized all his Provençal landscapes. Born at Aix, Cézanne spent his entire life in this corner of France, so favorable to painters, cut off, misunderstood by his contemporaries, completely devoting himself to a prophetic and splendid body of work which was to engender Cubism.

◀ Cézanne: "Mont Sainte-Victoire and the Black Castle."

SHRINES OF THE EUROPEAN GENIUS
BY FRANÇOIS FONTAINE

"Wherever the European spirit dominates, there can be seen the maximum need, the maximum effort... the maximum ambition, the maximum power, the maximum modification of external nature...." wrote Paul Valéry.

Every picture in this volume attests to the intensity with which the European nature is charged, and with which the men of this continent infuse their works. If the proof seems a bit forced, if these images seem to have been chosen for their exceptional qualities, we can only answer that they have been included for their exemplary character. The marvelous in Europe is never accidental. Sometimes it is unique—but it is not mysterious, not arbitrary—each man is free to trace its causes and then to retrace their effects. The marvelous takes such varied forms in Europe that its very profusion, which may cloy the observer, also justifies his saying: this is a masterpiece—yet it is only one example among many. And finally, the marvelous is generously distributed, both geographically and historically. It is the heritage of every European; it is what one is proudest of, and again it is what one most envies, or rather covets. The pleasure is twofold: one can show the traveler the treasures that do not exist in his own country, then go and see those that do.

So that, while wandering through this gallery of places and works, one sees it as both a limited catalogue of unique insights and a prospectus of the continent's infinite splendors. Is it the European genius or only the genius of a few places and a few artists that has been shown to us? Have these "maxima" really the meaning that Valéry gave them?

We must clear the matter up. The European spirit does not like misunderstandings, especially when it is a question of knowing exactly what that spirit is, and therefore what it can do. It is because it clearly assessed its own possibilities at each plateau of its evolution that it was able to accumulate, transmit, and surpass itself. If it had wallowed smugly in the unknowable, the intemporal, it would still be confined to that tiny cape of Asia which is its geographic definition. If it had ceased measuring itself with its own eyes, by its own gauge, it would have escaped the Far Eastern mass, only to lose itself in the Far Western mass where the machine is in serious competition with man. But what we are defining here is the spirit of a civilization, that is, an average with which everyone feels at home, and not maxima to which only a few have access. We therefore return to our question: is the European who knows himself and holds himself in check really so much at ease in this setting of wonders, or is he confused by the contrasts of nature; does he possess his creative genius, or does this same genius possess him?

The reply was given in the very first pages of this book, and at the dawn of our civilization. The wisdom of the ancients had made room for both means and extremes of the spirit. Or rather, some say, nature was then felt in such a way that the clarity and gentle swell of the seascape, contrasting with the aridity of the tormented earth, early accustomed man to the two aspects of his life: tension and moderation. This last characteristic of the Greek genius is so familiar to us that it hides the first. Protagoras is probably more typical of Europe than Prometheus. But if man has to be the measure of everything, this has no practical consequences unless he also wants to be, first and foremost, the master of everything. Where Prometheus failed, Apollo was to succeed. Because it was at Delphi that he wrestled with the serpent, Delphi was the high place of the world of antiquity; one learned there, and one still learns elsewhere, that there is in the order of intelligence, as in that of morals, a conflict between good and evil, light and shadow.

The Pythia is there to remind us of it. She goes into trances, for the serpent possesses her, but she pronounces the oracle of Apollo: "Know thyself." And the traveler who goes away with this message is a European.

But one must be able to interpret the oracle, and it is extraordinary that so few were mistaken in the West. In other regions of the world the difficulty of interpreting has been an excuse for avoiding action. On the shores of the Mediterranean, however lethargic those shores may seem, the Greeks set off in search of their own moral, physical and metaphysical nature; and one can see, two thousand five hundred years later, where such curiosity may lead. Solon, Euclid, Plato, Aristotle and Hippocrates are still the presiding geniuses in our universities, though they have ceased to be the teachers. They continue to furnish themes for research.

So, what we call literature is only a prolonged echo of the dialogue begun by Euripides between the individual and his fate. The first spectators heard at Epidaurus the first questions of the "character" in whom they recognized their anxieties, the character who accomplished before their eyes their glorious or frightful dreams and who died so that they could for a moment live more intensely. From then on, literature was a variant on this first theme.

Democracy also was to be born nearby. But it slowly wilted on the rock of the Acropolis and flourished anew in a younger land. Taking the city as its starting point, Rome succeeded in becoming an empire, but at the price of what efforts of juridical imagination! Every square foot of the Roman Forum has a history that can still be read in our modern constitutions and codes of civil law. There, Cicero made the *res publica* his property and gave it its life.

But it was already too large, and its life defined the life of the known world. The divine century of Augustus, the golden age of the Antonines . . . Greece furnished the teachers, the East furnished the religions. Soon one can no longer tell where the properly Roman element lies in the cosmopolitan capital of the Empire. Men from the eastern provinces, slaves or travelers entrusted with secret missions, go underground in a splendid and violent city to commune in poverty and peace.

In the catacombs a new Europe is born, of a tradition foreign to Greek rationalism and Roman materialism; it will impose itself on the barbarians when they have overrun the Empire. One can guess, less by its artifacts than by its inexhaustible spiritual radiation, the intensity of the underground life where the conquering Church was organized.

The Roman Empire collapsed, and if its relics were transported to Byzantium, its spirit remained in the ruins. Churchmen salvage what can be salvaged —Gregory the Great, St. Augustine, St. Boniface— while waiting to restore the fate of Europe to the temporal power. Finally, in Rome on Christmas night in the year 800, Charlemagne is crowned and consecrated and re-establishes the Empire of the West. But the center of gravity of the Christian world is to be among the successors, on the ancient boundaries of Roman power, at the starting point of barbarian vitality. The Nordic Caesar reigns from Aachen; there he will have his tomb and there will be perpetuated the memory of the first attempt at the unification of the European peoples.

The Europe of Charlemagne came too late to revive the legacy of Rome, and too early to institute a new order. It almost seems that the disintegration had to be total, and after Charlemagne we enter upon three centuries of feudalism, i.e., of anarchy tempered by the local discipline of lordlings and by the moral authority of the Church. This world is without aim; it has no future. It is ennobled by a spiritual and material adventure, the Crusades. Peter the Hermit raises the first troops of mystics and pillagers. St. Bernard tries to organize these foolish expeditions and officer them.

Can order also be allied to pure reason? Provoked by this question, St. Bernard immediately turns round to face a new danger: in Paris, a layman of extraordinary presumption, Abélard, dares to apply a critical intelligence to everything. Men come from everywhere to hear his incomparable dialectics. St. Bernard thinks he has crushed him by the superiority of his eloquence and above all by the authority of the Church. But it is Abélard who finally wins: the Sorbonne will perpetuate his free quest for knowledge. Every city in the West will have its university, from Coimbra to Louvain, from Oxford or Cambridge in England to Göttingen in Germany.

Aix-la-Chapelle   Charlemagne

Vézelay

Saint Francis of Assisi   Assisi

Chartres Cathedral

Yet Héloïse will end her days in the Convent of the Paraclete, one of the fifteen thousand Benedictine abbeys in Europe where were stored the literary treasures saved from the barbarian storm. In the eyes of the men of this period culture appeared inseparable from faith. Art also, from the most delicate miniature to the most audacious monument. The cathedral builders, at Chartres as at Amiens or Bourges, achieved a maximum; but would the European genius now fall into the excess in which so many other proud or foolishly mystic civilizations foundered prematurely? No, for gradually Europe became middle-class. With the return of security, trade began again; the Crusades at least communicated Eastern skills and refinement to this society of barely tamed barbarians which had just been emancipated from the great fear of the millennium. Cities of merchants claim liberties, including the freedom to administer their prosperity themselves. But all around great poverty still holds the field. The son of a rich Assisi merchant sheds his riches one fine morning and embraces this poverty where it is most rife. His example wins over a host of men who engage in the spiritual combat between penury and luxury, between natural simplicity and artificial riches. More than any other man, St. Francis restored hope to his century.

The nature in which the Mendicant Order plunges, that of the wolves and the birds, other men draw nearer to, less poetically but with equal ardor. Many pursue in it the opposite of poverty. While alchemists shut themselves up with their sterile research, an extraordinary Franciscan explores one by one the fruitful ways of science. In Roger Bacon, the Admirable Doctor, is expressed the practical genius of the peoples of the North that had been lacking in Latin antiquity.

Because Italy has never really lost contact with Byzantium, luxury and the arts make an earlier reappearance there. The luxury of political quarrels, in particular, is rife in the aristocracy that rules the cities. By accident, it gives birth to the first great work of art of modern times. Born a Guelph, exiled from Florence as a Ghibelline, Dante wanders all his life in the outer shadows; deprived of the love of his native city, as he had been of the love of Beatrice, he writes down the visions that no man had yet dared to express in words, and, what is more, in modern language. When he departs the world he vowed to the Inferno, the radiant Petrarch is already born and the Renaissance is nigh.

Literature takes flight, but how limited is its range! The privilege of a few, the rich possessors of a few books, it would never have been the leaven of civilization if a clever man, a talented contractor, had not brought about the technical miracle of its multiplication. Gutenberg made possible the diffusion of the Bible, but it is equally true that he secularized literature, no longer the prerogative of monk-copyists, and socialized literature, no longer the monopoly of the rich....

In effect, these immeasurable strokes of fortune are soon embodied in a few men of an intellectual breadth that has rarely been achieved, as if all the currents that had run underground since antiquity had converged and sprung up anew in a minute spot in Europe: Florence, the new Athens. It was there that Leonardo da Vinci and Michelangelo matured to greatness.

It is in other privileged places—privileged by their presence—that these universal geniuses will show what they are made of. Michelangelo astounds himself as he re-creates the world in frescoes, in marble, by poetry or in the ordering of the palaces on the Capitol. Leonardo explores all the possibilities of the mind. His search interests him more than his achievement—and even where he most excelled, in his painting.

Another wind, however, blew from northeastern France, where the Latin spirit had left fewer traces, where the Roman church had not assured its total ascendancy and where certain forms of political and spiritual autonomy were maintained. Would Rabelais' Gargantua have been possible in this atmosphere of free discussion animating the humanists of Rotterdam, exalting the reformer of Wittenberg? Erasmus, Luther and Calvin kindle in the Netherlands, Germany and Switzerland more than the hearths of culture: they set alight fires of the mind.

Too many certainties too suddenly challenged set Europe off balance. Factions tear one another apart. Frightened by the ravages of militant humanism, another humanism, more serene, more skeptical even, makes itself heard in a land of moderation: in his tower, Montaigne's "library" in Dordogne, the author of the famous *Essays* calms minds and invites them to more modesty in human opinions and works. And yet his attempt is one of the most ambitious, one of the proudest—some will say: the attempt of the man who wants to know himself, however disconcerting and nonconforming his discovery may be. And just as he is invited to explore his individual nature, the European is thrust into an unknown universe. Montaigne may take an interest in the customs of the American savages—but Cortès has already destroyed their civilization. The hour of Spanish Europe strikes in the Escorial where treasures from the Indies are piled up. It is no coincidence that a creative period accompanies this new fortune. Cervantes expresses at one stroke, for all time, the whole genius of a people. At the same time, El Greco immortalizes it in its almost unbearable grandeur. Already the Toledo sky is clouding over and the horizon is shrinking. Spain will retreat into herself. But the world is now immeasurably vaster. Europe in effect knows no more limits. And to

Dante

Florence

Michelangelo

Capitol Square, Rome

Chinon

Rabelais

El Greco

El Greco's House at Toledo

Elsinore Castle, Denmark

Shakespeare

Molière

Molière's armchair

Leipzig in the 18th century

J.-S. Bach

Pascal

Abbey of Port-Royal-des-Champs

cap it all she produces one of the richest and most profoundly human works that have ever been. At Stratford-on-Avon, from the brain of a single creator spring forth Prospero and Caliban, Romeo and Juliet, Hamlet and Lady Macbeth; Julius Caesar, Cleopatra and Henry V live again. In a few years the world is populated with more heroes and myths than in the preceding thousand: will literature follow the course in which Shakespeare's universal genius has launched it? No, for it cannot, without being unfaithful to the spirit of Europe, stray away from the measure it has set itself.

So today we must make an effort to remember that *The Tempest* is, chronologically speaking, a work of the seventeenth century. Prospero and Ariel left the memory of man for two centuries. Magicians no longer have any place in a world of logicians organized under the aegis of the French language and spirit. Literary genres are invented, the rules of drama are defined and an Academy is created. And yet these disciplines and this conformity do not stifle genius. Molière and Racine cheat with the classical ideal: *Don Juan* and *Phèdre* go back to the old Dionysiac foundation, and the ridiculous but delectable *Malade Imaginaire* will be the last part played by Molière. La Fontaine is an island of green in this artificial civilization. But the rod is a rod of iron, and literature becomes an institution, a spiritual architecture. The theater once more becomes the temple of old.

What is called the *Grand Siècle* is in parts immense. It is faithful to the classical spirit in the arts, raised by the choirmaster of St. Thomas' in Leipzig, Johann Sebastian Bach, to heights that can be measured only from a great distance. But it is foreign to that spirit, in some ways alien to the century, where metaphysics are concerned: Descartes and his whirlwinds, Leibnitz and his infinitesimals, and above all Pascal, whose anguish is common to all ages—but less perhaps to the age he lived in than any other. Port-Royal, a landmark of nonconformism that became intolerable in a century so obsessed with order, contained more soul than Versailles, and its Solitaries defied the greatest court in Europe. This court will swarm with art, and other great kings will want to have court writers. But Voltaire is stifled at the court of King Frederick, and Diderot resists the entreaties of Catherine the Great. Soon the spirit will find liberty in certain places of refuge: Geneva becomes a den of original and seditious thought. Rousseau lives there less uncomfortably than elsewhere—but he formed his strange genius there. Voltaire finds himself safer there than in Paris—of which he expresses, however, the vivacity and the insolence. We might really believe that a new European civilization, its mother spirit the literary language that is French, is about to be born. It is the golden age of writers. Yet the creative genius who dominates this period has to struggle to exist, and dies in abject poverty. The eighteenth century cannot be forgiven for not knowing that Salzburg was its true spiritual capital.

The fall of the Bastille troubles Kant's walks, Valmy upsets Goethe, Marengo inspires Beethoven who, already in his native Bonn, was conscious of the first symptoms of the imminent upheaval. France stirs, expends her substance disproportionately, Germany reflects, incubates Romanticism, and peoples dream of independence and revolution. Faust really will win. He has conquered the soul of Europe which, for its part, will at last assure him possession of the world.

Where are the shrines of the nineteenth century? In the workshop where Fulton is preparing for the mechanical civilization, in the room where Proudhon is announcing the social consequences of this civilization? At Missolonghi where Byron is fighting for liberty, in Guernsey where Victor Hugo is defying the imperial régime? In the laboratory where Pasteur is discovering disease germs? At Bayreuth where Wagner is orchestrating the old Germanic dreams? This century, of which we are the descendants, is full of bristling peaks that still obscure our vision of the past, and hamper us from taking a just measure of the present.

Never had the will to dominate nature, to reconstruct the world, obsessed man with so much intensity. It was then that extremes of boldness and ambition were achieved by the European. What the world is today, our grandfathers forged. Yet little by little their most powerful visions ceased to be realized on the very continent where they had been conceived, so much did rivalries and national wars bring ruins and waste of energy. Today we have seen the decline of Europe; perhaps it was fleetingly tempted, in a movement of proud withdrawal, to organize itself as a museum. That would have been another way of educating the universe....

But it was decreed that the Hellenistic experiment should not be repeated, that a just degree of political power and a just degree of economic well-being had become the conditions necessary to the creative spirit in the modern world. Europe understood just in time, in the middle of the twentieth century, that it would need a reunion of all its forces to continue to create. To accept the challenge of progress, it has pooled its resources and its men. In the maximum space, with the maximum spiritual and material possibilities, with what new wonders will the genius of our peoples not enrich the European treasure-house!

F. F.

J.-J. Rousseau

Lake of Geneva

Beethoven's birthplace in Bonn

Beethoven

Victor Hugo

Hugo's house in Guernsey

Bayreuth Theater

Wagner

THE PHOTOGRAPHS IN THIS VOLUME ARE BY:

AEROFILMS LTD, I. AISTRUP, ALINARI, ALMASY, ICELANDIC EMBASSY IN PARIS, ANDERSON, O. ANGERMAYER, ASSOCIATED PRESS,

BARRINGTON BROWN, J. M. BAUFLE, BAYREUTHER FESTSPIELE, P. BELZEAUX, G. BERENGO-GARDIN, BERINGER AND PAMPALUCHI, F. BERKO, H. BERTAULT, BIBLIOTHÈQUE NATIONALE, W. BISCHOF, BOISSONNAS, J. BOTTIN, E. BOUBAT, E. BOUDOT-LAMOTTE, B. BRANDT, BROMPTON STUDIOS, BRASSAI, D. BUDNIK, BULLOZ, R. BURRI, H. BUSCH,

J. LE CAISNE, H. CARTIER-BRESSON, J. P. CHARBONNIER, CICCIONE, F. CLAES, A. CONTAMINE, A. COURTEVILLE,

R. DELVERT, K. DEJMO, R. DESCHARNES, M. DESJARDINS, C. DESSART, DRAEGER, J. DUBOIS,

G. EHRMANN, H. ELKAN,

J. FAGE, E. FIEGER, FLIEGER UND FLABDIENST, B. FRANSIOLI, L. FRÉDÉRIC, A. FREQUIN, T. FREY, J. FRONVAL,

J. GABERELL G. GRUPI, E. GÉRIN, GHEDINA, GIRAUDON, GOURSAT, GUILLEMOT, K. GULLERS,

H. HAMMARSKIOLD, D. HARISSIADIS, W. F. V. HEEMSKERCK-DUKER, A. HELD, F. HENLE, HENRARD, L. HENRI, T. HOLLYMAN, HOLMES-LEBEL, FRENCH NATIONAL GEOGRAPHICAL INSTITUTE, I. IOANNIDES, L. IONESCO,

L. JAHAN, H. JEANBRAU,

KIPA, KLM, AEROCARTO N. V.

A. LAMMER, J. A. LAVAUD, C. LÉNARS, E. LESSING, W. LIMOT, LOEBL,

MACHATSCHEK, G. MAIRANI, ANDRÉ MARTIN, GEORGES MARTIN, G. MASSON, L. VON MATT, MILLET, MITTET FOTO, G. DE MIRÉ, P. MOLINARD, MONDADORI-PRESS, B. MOOSBRUGGER, I. MORATH,

NADAR, R. NADAU, NATIONALMUSEUM STOCKHOLM, DR. NAWRATH, STUDIO NERVI, J. NETTIS, J. NIEPCE, P. N. NILSON, NORSK POLARINSTITUT, H. NULL, SWISS NATIONAL TOURIST OFFICE, BRITISH TOURIST OFFICE, C. OORTHUYS,

M. PAVLOVIC, H. PEDONE, VUES AÉRIENNES PERCEVAL, G. PÉTREMAND, O. PFEIFER, K. PLICKA,

E. RENNER, M. RIBOUD, RICHARD-BLIN, ROGER VIOLLET, F. ROITER, W. RONIS, C. ROTKIN, J. ROUBIER,

S. DE SAZO, SCALA, T. SCHNEIDERS, M. SERRAILLIER, J. G. SERUZIER, D. SEYMOUR, H. SIBLEY, G. SILBERSTEIN, H. W. SILVESTER, EDWIN SMITH, EUGÈNE SMITH, J. L. STAGE, D. STANIMIROVITCH, W. SUSCHITZKY, J. L. SWINERS, SWISSAIR,

K. TACONIS, P. TAIRRAZ, N. TREATTY, R. TRUCHON,

O. VARING FOTO, H. VAUPEL, G. VIENNE, A. VIGNEAU, VONK,

S. WEISS, WIDEROES FLYVESELSKAP A.S., R. WINQUIST, WOLF AND TRITSCHLER, YAN.

LIST OF ILLUSTRATIONS

Molière's Chair at the Comédie-Française, Paris (M. Desjardins, Réalités)
Leipzig in the 18th century (Bibliotheque Nationale)
J.-S. Bach, Anonymous Portrait (Giraudon)
Abbey of Port-Royal-des-Champs, France (L. Henri, Rapho)
J.-J. Rousseau, after Albrier (Giraudon)   329
Lake Geneva, Switzerland (B. Fransioli)
Beethoven's birthplace in Bonn, Germany (A. Courteville, Réalités)
Beethoven (Vonk)
Victor Hugo (Nadar)
Victor Hugo's house in Guernsey (British Tourist Office)
Bayreuth Theater, Germany (Bayreuther Festspiele)
Wagner (Bayreuther Festspiele)

* Asterisks refer to color illustrations.

JACKET: The Acropolis, Athens (J.-A. Lavaud). Strasbourg Cathedral (J. Fronval). Stained-glass window, Chartres Cathedral (J. Fronval). St. Mark's, Venice (G. Berengo-Gardin). Botticelli's "Allegory of Spring" (R. Descharnes).

END-PAPERS: "The Rape of Europe" by Nicholas Poussin (detail).
Copyright Stadmuseet, Stockholm.

THIS WORK, THE SECOND TO BE PUBLISHED
IN THE RÉALITÉS COLLECTION,
DIRECTED BY PIERRE LEVALLOIS AND GASTON D'ANGÉLIS,
WAS PLANNED WITH THE COLLABORATION
OF FRANÇOIS FONTAINE, ANDRÉ LAMY, DANIELLE HUNEBELLE AND EDMOND POGNON,
AND PRODUCED BY SOLANGE ROBINET (LAYOUT);
MARIE-THÉRÈSE GRIFFOUL (PHOTOGRAPHIC MATERIAL),
FRANÇOISE BIRO, JOSETTE CONTRÉRAS, ALAIN HERVÉ, JACQUELINE SIEGER (CAPTIONS);
LAMBERT TERBRACK (EDITORIAL SECRETARIAT).

PRINTED IN FRANCE BY THE IMPRIMERIES DE BOBIGNY,
ON "LE REVARD" PHOTOGRAVURE PAPER OF THE PAPETERIES DE SAVOIE.